Garbage and Recycling

Peggy J. Parks

Energy and the Environment

ReferencePoint
Press®

San Diego, CA

About the Author

Peggy J. Parks holds a bachelor of science degree from Aquinas College in Grand Rapids, Michigan, where she graduated magna cum laude. She has written more than 90 nonfiction educational books for children and young adults, Parks lives in Muskegon, Michigan, a town that she says inspires her writing because of its location on the shores of Lake Michigan.

© 2011 ReferencePoint Press, Inc.

For more information, contact:
ReferencePoint Press, Inc.
PO Box 27779
San Diego, CA 92198
www. ReferencePointPress.com

Picture credits:
Cover: Dreamstime and iStockphoto.com
Maury Aaseng: 32–34, 47–49, 63–65, 77–78
AP Images: 13
iStockphoto.com: 15

LIBRARY OF CONGRESS CATALOGING-IN-PUBLICATION DATA

Parks, Peggy J., 1951–
  Garbage and recycling / by Peggy J. Parks.
    p. cm. — (Compact research)
  Includes bibliographical references and index.
  ISBN-13: 978-1-60152-121-7 (hardback)
  ISBN-10: 1-60152-121-9 (hardback)
  1. Refuse and refuse disposal—Juvenile literature. 2. Recycling (Waste, etc.)—Juvenile literature. I. Title.
  TD792.P375 2011
  363.72'8—dc22

                                                                        2010013881

Contents

Foreword

As modern civilization continues to evolve, its ability to create, store, distribute, and access information expands exponentially. The explosion of information from all media continues to increase at a phenomenal rate. By 2020 some experts predict the worldwide information base will double every 73 days. While access to diverse sources of information and perspectives is paramount to any democratic society, information alone cannot help people gain knowledge and understanding. Information must be organized and presented clearly and succinctly in order to be understood. The challenge in the digital age becomes not the creation of information, but how best to sort, organize, enhance, and present information.

ReferencePoint Press developed the *Compact Research* series with this challenge of the information age in mind. More than any other subject area today, researching current issues can yield vast, diverse, and unqualified information that can be intimidating and overwhelming for even the most advanced and motivated researcher. The *Compact Research* series offers a compact, relevant, intelligent, and conveniently organized collection of information covering a variety of current topics ranging from illegal immigration and deforestation to diseases such as anorexia and meningitis.

The series focuses on three types of information: objective single-author narratives, opinion-based primary source quotations, and facts and statistics. The clearly written objective narratives provide context and reliable background information. Primary source quotes are carefully selected and cited, exposing the reader to differing points of view. And facts and statistics sections aid the reader in evaluating perspectives. Presenting these key types of information creates a richer, more balanced learning experience.

For better understanding and convenience, the series enhances information by organizing it into narrower topics and adding design features that make it easy for a reader to identify desired content. For example, in *Compact Research: Illegal Immigration*, a chapter covering the economic impact of illegal immigration has an objective narrative explaining the various ways the economy is impacted, a balanced section of numerous primary source quotes on the topic, followed by facts and full-color illustrations to encourage evaluation of contrasting perspectives.

The ancient Roman philosopher Lucius Annaeus Seneca wrote, "It is quality rather than quantity that matters." More than just a collection of content, the *Compact Research* series is simply committed to creating, finding, organizing, and presenting the most relevant and appropriate amount of information on a current topic in a user-friendly style that invites, intrigues, and fosters understanding.

Garbage and Recycling at a Glance

What Constitutes Garbage

The most basic way to define garbage, waste, or trash is anything that is thrown away because it is no longer wanted or needed.

Garbage Generation

Individuals, businesses, organizations, industries, institutions, and all other entities produce some kind of waste. By far, the greatest volume of garbage is generated by industries.

Seriousness of Garbage Problem

The U.S. Environmental Protection Agency states that waste production totaled 250 million tons (227 million metric tons) in 2008, and as the population has grown, the volume of waste has continued to increase.

Landfill Capacity

Although landfill capacity has remained relatively constant over the last few decades, space for garbage disposal is expected to run out in approximately 20 years based on present waste generation rates.

Incinerating Garbage

Burning trash instead of burying it conserves landfill space, but incineration emits toxic substances such as dioxins and heavy metals into the atmosphere. Modern incineration plants emit fewer toxins, and many generate fuel and electricity from garbage.

Threats to Oceans

Plastic debris, used oil, discarded fishing nets, and other waste in the ocean has caused serious pollution and poses a grave threat to marine life.

Toxic Garbage

When used oil, antifreeze, batteries, household cleaners, prescription medicines, and medical/pharmaceutical waste are not disposed of properly, they can pollute soil and groundwater.

E-Waste

As the demand for computers, printers, cell phones, and other electronic equipment has skyrocketed, massive volumes of e-waste are being generated. These devices contain numerous toxic materials that, if improperly disposed of, can pollute soil and groundwater.

Benefits of Recycling

Recycling diverts enormous amounts of waste from landfills and saves natural resources and energy when products are made from recyclables rather than virgin materials.

Garbage Reduction in the Future

Individuals and businesses are decreasing the amount of garbage they produce through reduction, reuse, and recycling, while plasma gasification plants vaporize garbage to generate fuel and electricity.

Overview

Overview

66 Every year, Americans throw away some 100 billion plastic bags after they've been used to transport a prescription home from the drugstore or a quart of milk from the grocery store. It's equivalent to dumping nearly 12 million barrels of oil. 99

—Katharine Mieszkowski, a senior writer for *Salon* who covers science and environmental issues.

66 Driving into work today, I saw garbage bins overflowing and city dumpsters spilling out with trash. It stinks. It's disgusting. It's uncivilized. It's probably dangerous to some extent. 99

—Jeffrey A. Tucker, who is with the economics and libertarian group Ludwig von Mises Institute.

With more than 8 million people, New York is the largest city in the United States—and the largest producer of garbage. Together the residents, businesses, schools, hotels, restaurants, and construction operations in the city's 5 boroughs of Manhattan, Brooklyn, the Bronx, Queens, and Staten Island generate as much as 36,200 tons (33,000 metric tons) of trash every day, which totals more than 13 million tons (12 million metric tons) per year. As journalist Steve Cohen writes: "Why do New Yorkers create so much garbage? Well there are a lot of us and New Yorkers are busy people—we toss garbage casually and we don't like to sort our garbage. We prefer not to think about garbage or where it will end up. I think we have this fantasy that those green plastic mounds of garbage bags on the street are magically transported to some mythical solid waste heaven."[1]

Adding to the challenge of such an immense amount of garbage is that all New York City landfills are now closed, so trash must be transported to landfills or incinerators in Virginia, Pennsylvania, Ohio, New Jersey, and South Carolina. Although some garbage is carried on trains and barges, most is trucked, which takes a heavy toll on the environment. Cohen explains:

> It is hard to imagine a more environmentally damaging waste-management system than the one we have in New York. . . . Today, we collect garbage with trucks that use high-polluting diesel fuel and then dump the garbage onto the floor of waste transfer stations that are typically located in poor neighborhoods. We then scoop the garbage up off the floor and load it onto large trucks that also burn high-polluting diesel fuel and ship it to landfills and waste to energy incinerators located away from New York City.[2]

It is crucial, says Cohen, for public policy to be developed that addresses New York's garbage problem, including waste reduction and recycling programs.

Mountains of Junk

The simplest definition of garbage is anything that is no longer wanted or needed and is thrown away. Garbage is generated by innumerable sources, including industrial operations and manufacturers; hotels, restaurants, and resorts; schools and hospitals; freighters and cruise ships; construction firms; and private residences—basically, any entity that exists produces some type of waste. As the global population has steadily risen, more than doubling since 1960, the world's garbage has grown exponentially. According to the environmental group Earth911, China and India have some of the world's worst garbage problems, caused

> " Garbage is generated by innumerable sources, including industrial operations and manufacturers; hotels, restaurants, and resorts; schools and hospitals; freighters and cruise ships; construction firms; and private residences—basically, any entity that exists produces some type of waste. "

by a combination of rapid population growth and poor waste management systems. Another country that struggles with garbage is Britain, which sends more waste to landfills than any country in Europe. If garbage generation continues to increase as it has been, all of Britain's landfills are expected to be filled to capacity before 2020.

The United States has also seen an enormous spike in garbage production over the years. According to the Environmental Protection Agency (EPA), waste production nearly tripled from 1960 to 2008, increasing from 88 million tons (80 million metric tons) to 250 million tons (227 million metric tons). Of all the types of garbage that contribute to America's total waste generation, paper constitutes the largest amount. This includes product packaging, office paper, junk mail, telephone books, paper grocery sacks, newspapers and magazines, and cardboard boxes. A close second to paper is yard waste and food scraps, followed by plastic, aluminum and other metals, rubber, leather, textiles, wood, and glass.

How Serious a Problem Is Garbage?

Although growing numbers of communities in the United States are implementing recycling programs, most garbage, including recyclable items, is thrown in the trash, which means it ends up in landfills. The EPA states that about 135 million tons (122 million metric tons) of waste was deposited into landfills in 2008, with the remainder being recycled or incinerated. Over the years, the number of landfills in the United States has shrunk dramatically, either because they were full or they failed to meet environmental regulatory standards. Newer landfills tend to be much larger than old ones; the Apex Regional Landfill in Las Vegas, Nevada, for instance, is the largest landfill in the country at 12,000 acres (4,856 hectares). So although there are fewer landfills, overall capacity has remained relatively constant. If garbage continues to be produced at the current rate, however, space will eventually run out. According to the National Solid Wastes Management Association, America has about 20 years of disposal capacity left in its landfills..

One of the most obvious problems caused by massive amounts of garbage is that it piles up and is unsightly as well as foul smelling, and it attracts disease-carrying rodents such as rats. This is a serious problem in large, populous cities such as New York, especially in the Bronx area, where the rat infestation is three times worse than in Manhattan and eight times worse than in Brooklyn. According to a New York pest control group, "A bad combination of vacant buildings, lots filled with overgrown weeds and unsealed trash containers has added up to a haven for rats."[3] Rats carry serious bacterial diseases such as leptospirosis, which can cause high fever, severe headaches, chills, vomiting, and diarrhea. If not treated, leptospirosis can lead to kidney damage, meningitis, liver failure, respiratory distress, and in rare cases, death.

When Garbage Is Burned

According to the EPA, the United States incinerates from 12 to 14 percent of its solid waste. Disposal of garbage in this way saves an immense amount of landfill space, but it is of concern to environmental groups because of toxic emissions that are produced during the burning process. Greenpeace states that incineration emits dioxins, heavy metals, and a number of other poisonous substances that pollute the air, soil, and water. This is a serious problem in China, where garbage production outpaces landfill capacity by at least 10 percent a year. Because of the country's overflowing landfills, increasing amounts of trash are being burned. In Shenzhen, a city in southeastern China, two enormous incinerators burn an estimated 40 percent of the region's garbage. According to an August 2009 *New York Times* report, the facilities "can be smelled a mile away and pour out so much dark smoke and hazardous chemicals that hundreds of local residents recently staged an all-day sit-in, demanding that the incinerators be cleaner and that a planned third incinerator not be built nearby."[4]

Yet not all incinerators are as polluting as those in Shenzhen. Newer models, many of which are waste-to-energy plants that create fuel or electricity from garbage, are often fitted with pollution-control devices that minimize toxic emissions. In an April 2010 article in the *New York Times*, journalist Elisabeth Rosenthal describes such facilities: "Today's

> " One of the most obvious problems caused by massive amounts of garbage is that it piles up and is unsightly as well as foul smelling, and it attracts disease-carrying rodents such as rats. "

new waste-to-energy plants contain a series of filters and scrubbers that remove almost all of the offending pollution, and older incinerators here have been retrofitted with these new devices. The pollution and emissions control systems take up almost as much floor space as the incinerators themselves."[5]

Oceans in Peril

Environmental groups and others who study earth's oceans warn that these vast bodies of water are becoming seriously polluted by garbage. Cruise ships are among the biggest polluters because the vessels—many of which are so massive that they are often called "floating cities"—can legally dump much of their garbage into the ocean as long as they are farther than three miles (4.8k) from shore. In addition to millions of gallons of raw sewage, these ships may dump food garbage, and even metal, paper, and glass, into the ocean as long as all the waste is ground into small pieces first. The only type of garbage that ships are prohibited from dumping is plastic, although the law is difficult to enforce when the vessels are far out at sea.

No matter how garbage ends up in the ocean, it poses a grave threat to marine life. One of the most serious dangers is the growing number of discarded plastic fishing nets, as a September 2009 article on the Mother Nature Network Web site explains: "The nets entangle seals, sea turtles and other animals in a phenomenon known as 'ghost fishing,' often drowning them. With more fishermen from developing countries now using plastic for its low cost and high durability, many abandoned nets can continue fishing on their own for months or years."[6] Another serious hazard for marine life is plastic rings that hold bottled or canned beverages together. When the rings end up in the ocean—and millions do every year—they can wrap around young creatures' necks and strangle them to death as their bodies grow.

Is Toxic Garbage a Serious Problem?

Toxic garbage is any form of waste that pollutes soil and water and is potentially harmful to humans and wildlife. One category, which the EPA calls universal waste, includes batteries, pesticides, mercury-containing equipment, and mercury-containing lightbulbs—all of which contain highly toxic chemicals. Other kinds of household toxic garbage include oven and

Discarded fishing nets often entangle and drown sea creatures such as this turtle, photographed near Hawaii. The Pacific is also home to a swirling mass of garbage thought to be twice the size of Texas, an area sometimes called the Great Pacific Garbage Patch.

drain cleaners, paint and paint thinners, antifreeze, wood and metal polishes, and various types of glues. When these and other forms of toxic garbage are disposed of in trash cans, they invariably end up in landfills.

Over time the poisons leak out of the waste and combine with rainwater to create a toxic liquid known as leachate. If leachate seeps through weak spots in landfill liners, it can pollute soil, surface water, and ground-water. But even when it is collected in special holding ponds, accidental spills can lead to pollution. In 2008 the owner of the largest landfill in Virginia was ordered to pay nearly $15,000 in fines for a spill two years before that sent 8,000 gallons (30,000L) of leachate into wetlands. The spill occurred after a truck driver, who was pumping the leachate from the landfill into a tanker truck, fell asleep.

Used motor oil is a particularly toxic form of waste, as it contains concentrations of heavy metals and chemicals such as arsenic, zinc, lead, chlorides, cadmium, and PCBs. Although the practice is illegal, many people who change the oil in their vehicles dispose of it improperly by dumping it on the ground or pouring it down drains or into storm sewers. The oil washes into waterways and is a major source of water contamination—in fact, the EPA states that used motor oil is the largest single source of oil pollution in lakes, rivers, and streams. To illustrate how grave this problem is, the used oil from just one oil change can contaminate 1 million gallons (3.8 million L) of fresh water.

> **Among the most toxic garbage sources is electronic waste, or e-waste, and the problem is rapidly growing worse.**

The Scourge of E-Waste

Among the most toxic garbage sources is electronic waste, or e-waste, and the problem is rapidly growing worse. As technology becomes more sophisticated, electronic equipment such as computers, printers, scanners, cell phones, televisions, DVD players, and digital cameras quickly becomes outdated, and people are eager to own the latest models. Many of their used devices are either in working order or are repairable and could be donated and reused by others. Most of the time, however, old electronics are thrown out and end up in landfills. This poses a serious pollution problem for the waste stream because electronic devices contain several hundred different materials, including heavy metals such as lead, mercury, and cadmium. For example, the cathode-ray tubes in just one television or computer monitor contain more than four pounds (1.81kg) of lead, as well as mercury and other toxins. As with all toxic substances, those contained in e-waste can leach out of landfills and con-taminate soil and groundwater.

A Three-Pronged Approach

When considering how to reduce the immense volume of garbage that ends up in landfills, recycling is often the first thing that many people think about. Numerous items can be recycled, including plastic and glass bottles; aluminum and steel cans; newspapers, magazines, and telephone

A crane operator sorts a mound of paper and cardboard for recycling. Recycling diverts enormous amounts of waste from landfills.

books; office paper; junk mail; and cardboard boxes. Yard waste such as leaves, twigs, and grass clippings, as well as food scraps, can be recycled into rich, organic fertilizer known as compost.

> **Even though recycling removes a significant amount of garbage from the waste stream, two other measures are equally important: source reduction and reuse.**

Yet even though recycling removes a significant amount of garbage from the waste stream, two other measures are equally important: source reduction and reuse. Together with recycling, these are known as the three Rs. Reduction involves creating less waste up front, such as making product packaging lighter and/or biodegradable. And just as the name implies, reuse involves giving away articles such as appliances, furniture, carpeting, clothing, and other articles, so they can be used by someone else. To encourage people to donate unwanted articles rather than throwing them out, groups have formed for the purpose of facilitating the exchange of reusable items. The largest of these groups is Freecycle, which is a grassroots organization that has nearly 8 million members in 85 countries.

How Effective Is Recycling?

The EPA states that as garbage generation has steadily grown over the years, the recycling rate has also increased. Nearly 83 million tons (75 million metric tons) of waste was recycled in 2008, compared to 5.6 million tons (5.08 million metric tons) in 1960. There are many benefits of recycling, the most obvious being that less garbage ends up in landfills. Recycling also conserves natural resources, because when recycled materials are used to manufacture new products, less virgin materials are needed, such as trees for paper production, bauxite to produce aluminum products, and silica for making glass. Another significant benefit of recycling is that it saves energy. According to the National Solid Wastes Management Association, the energy saved each year by steel recycling is equal to the electrical power used by 18 million homes. Recycling aluminum cans saves more than 90 percent of the energy needed to produce aluminum from bauxite ore. And the EPA adds that recycling benefits the environment because it "reduces air and water pollution associated with making new products from raw materials."[7]

Recycling has proved to be beneficial for numerous reasons, but there are also challenges associated with it. For one thing, people can become complacent about recycling, thinking that it does not matter how much waste they generate as long as much of it is recycled. Instead, the main focus should be on reducing the amount of garbage that is produced in the first place. Another hurdle is that many communities do not offer curbside pickup of recyclables. Because people may find it inconvenient to drive to recycling processing centers, many products that could be recycled end up as trash instead. As recycling continues to grow in popularity and its benefits become more attractive to communities and residents, these challenges may be overcome.

A Model City

Communities throughout the United States are becoming more environmentally conscious and are taking steps to reduce, reuse, and recycle waste products. San Francisco, California, has one of the country's most aggressive recycling programs. Homes, restaurants, hotels, and businesses are furnished with three color-coded carts: blue for paper, glass, plastics, metal, and other recyclables; green for food and yard waste; and black for trash that is destined for the landfill. Charges are on a "pay-as-you-throw" basis, meaning the less trash people throw out for the landfill, the less money they pay for garbage pickup. Currently an estimated 72 percent of San Francisco's garbage is diverted away from landfills, which is more than any other community in the United States—yet city officials vow to do better. They have an aggressive goal of reducing waste so that none of it ends up in landfills by the year 2020.

A key component of San Francisco's recycling initiative is its composting program, which became mandatory for all residents in October 2009. City trash haulers pick up organic waste from the green bins and transport it to a composting facility, where the waste is ground up and packed tightly into enormous plastic bags. The organic material begins to decompose, and over a period of time it changes into compost. During an average year about 105,000 tons (95,250 metric tons) of food scraps and yard trimmings are turned into an estimated 20,000 tons (18,144 metric tons) of dark, nutrient-rich compost, which is then sold. Each year, the compost is plentiful enough to cover about 10,000 acres (4,046.9 hectares) of land, and it is a coveted fertilizer for farmers and vineyard owners. As an April 2009 article in the *San Francisco Chronicle* explains: "The compost is in such demand from nearby growers of wine grapes, vegetables and nuts that it sells out at peak spreading season every year."[8]

How Can Garbage Be Reduced in the Future?

Although landfill space is relatively plentiful in the United States, this will not last forever—ways to reduce, reuse, and recycle trash will become even more critical in the coming years. One of the most aggressive solutions for solving the garbage problem is known as zero waste, and the idea behind it is simple: If something can potentially be reused, it should never be thrown away—and if it does not have a second use, it should not exist in the first place. The Berkeley Ecology Center, a West Coast leader in the zero-waste movement, explains: "If it can't be reduced, reused, repaired, rebuilt, refurbished, refinished, resold, recycled or composted, then it should be restricted, redesigned or removed from production."[9]

> Although landfill space is relatively plentiful in the United States, this will not last forever—ways to reduce, reuse, and recycle trash will become even more critical in the coming years.

Other garbage reduction measures are also being explored, such as burning more garbage in waste-to-energy incinerators. Another promising option for the future is a sophisticated form of technology known as plasma gasification. This process involves heating garbage to super-hot temperatures, which vaporizes it and creates a synthetic fuel called syngas. The syngas can be burned to generate electricity, or it can be converted into fuels such as gasoline and ethanol. As Westinghouse Plasma Corporation explains:

In the plasma gasification process, heat nearly as hot as the sun's surface is used to break down the molecular structure of any carbon-containing materials—such as municipal solid waste (MSW), tires, hazardous waste, biomass, river sediment, coal and petroleum coke—and convert them into synthesis gas (syngas) that can be used to generate power, liquids fuels or other sustainable sources of energy.[10]

Meeting the Challenges

The global population rose from 3 billion in 1960 to nearly 7 billion in 2010, and over the same period of time, the amount of garbage has grown exponentially. This has forced countries throughout the world to find better disposal methods, and even more importantly, to reduce the amount of garbage that is generated.

How Serious a Problem Is Garbage?

66 **Our trash, or municipal solid waste (MSW), is made up of the things we commonly use and then throw away. These materials range from packaging, food scraps, and grass clippings, to old sofas, computers, tires, and refrigerators.** 99

—U.S. Environmental Protection Agency, whose mission is to protect human health and the environment.

66 **There's waste that comes from doing something that manifestly doesn't need doing. A hundred million trees are cut every year just to satisfy the junk-mail industry.** 99

—Bill McKibben, cofounder of the environmental movement 350.org
and the author of *Earth: Making a Life in a Tough New World.*

Naples, a city in southern Italy, has long been known for its rich history as well as its art, culture, music, and architecture. It is also famous for its Neapolitan cuisine and holds the distinction of being the birthplace of pizza. Nestled into the shoreline of a picturesque bay, Naples offers breathtaking views of the Mediterranean Sea and the towering Mount Vesuvius, and it is often called one of Italy's most beautiful, vibrant cities. Yet there is another side to Naples that is anything *but* beautiful.

Naples had struggled with burgeoning amounts of garbage for more than a decade; this problem reached a crisis point in December 2007. Overflowing landfills were closed to further dumping, and enormous heaps of trash, some as high as the upper floors of buildings, filled city streets. By the following May, garbage was piling up at the rate of more than 7,000 tons (6,350 metric tons) per day. The situation became so dire that some residents were setting the garbage on fire, creating a noxious, putrid-smelling inferno. A March 2010 article in *Spiegel International* describes this chaos: "Plastic bags filled with garbage covered the Piazza del Plebiscito in Naples. In the suburbs, piles of garbage grew like tumors along arterial roads, and at night the air was heavy with the pungent odor of burning dumps."[11]

As the garbage crisis continued to worsen in Naples, Italian officials became desperate for a way to resolve it. They reopened a few landfills, built several new incinerators, and called in the army to help move the piles of trash out of the streets. They also began sending entire trainloads of garbage to Germany, where it was incinerated in waste-to-energy plants. This was only a temporary solution, however, as the director of two incineration plants in Hamburg, Germany, explains: "We are doing this because we were asked to provide emergency aid, but we will do it only for a few months, not years. This is not a long-term solution. Italy will have to solve Italy's problem."[12] In March 2010 the European Union declared that Italian officials had still not adopted adequate measures to dispose of garbage to keep it from endangering the environment and human health.

Garbage, Garbage, and More Garbage

Naples is not the only city in Italy that has serious garbage problems. Much of the country struggles with the same problem primarily because of its reliance on landfills for disposal of more than 60 percent of its trash. That is only slightly higher than the United States, which sends 54 percent of its waste to landfills, but there is one crucial difference. Italy, which consists of only 116,300 square miles (301,216 sq. km), has very little disposal space left, while the United States, at 3.5 million square miles (9.06 million sq. km), has more than 1,700 operating landfills, many of which are massive. According to the National Solid Wastes Management Association, the United States has enough disposal capacity to last for at least 20 more years. That is

> **Landfills throughout the world are repositories for every type of garbage imaginable.**

an average, however, as some states have enough landfill space to accommodate decades' worth of garbage, while others have little or no disposal capacity left and must transport garbage elsewhere.

Landfills throughout the world are repositories for every type of garbage imaginable. In the United States the EPA monitors waste by tracking how much is generated and what types of garbage people throw away. The agency states that every year, people in the United States dispose of 16 billion disposable diapers, 2 billion razors, 1 billion foil-lined fruit juice boxes, 2 billion used batteries, 25 billion Styrofoam cups, and 1.6 billion disposable pens, much of which ends up in landfills. In addition, thousands of old televisions are dumped in landfills, as are junked cars, worn-out mattresses, pieces of carpeting, tires, sofas, chairs, and appliances.

> "
>
> The [Environmental Protection Agency] states that every year, people in the United States dispose of 16 billion disposable diapers, 2 billion razors, 1 billion foil-lined fruit juice boxes, 2 billion used batteries, 25 billion Styrofoam cups, and 1.6 billion disposable pens, much of which ends up in landfills.
>
> "

What Happens to Buried Garbage?

Garbage decomposes at different rates based on how biodegradable it is. For example, food and yard waste break down within a few weeks, while disposable diapers and Styrofoam cups can last for hundreds of years. As the EPA explains: "Even 500 years from now, the foam coffee cup you used this morning will be sitting in a landfill."[13] Yet although organic material biodegrades far more quickly than Styrofoam, metal, or glass, even food scraps and yard clippings may last for decades when they are buried in landfills. In order to understand why this is, it is important to know what takes place during decomposition.

Living organisms such as microbes and enzymes "eat" the garbage, which begins the biodegradation process. This occurs much more rapidly under aerobic conditions, meaning that oxygen is present to help break the molecules of the substances apart. But because landfills compact garbage so tightly and then bury it, air cannot reach the waste. Under these anaerobic conditions, garbage decomposes very, very slowly. This became evident during a study by researchers from the University of Arizona who excavated landfills throughout North America. They found hundreds of foods such as hot dogs, grapes, and lettuce, as well as more than 2,400 newspapers that were still readable. From the dates on the newspapers, the researchers could tell that the food was about 40 years old—and in all that time, it had not decomposed.

Garbage Gas

Although food and yard waste can be recycled into compost, much of this organic material ends up in landfills. According to the EPA, an estimated 33 million tons (30 million metric tons) of yard waste and 31 million tons (28 million metric tons) of food scraps were deposited in landfills during 2008. When organic waste decomposes under anaerobic conditions, several types of gas are formed. One, known as hydrogen sulfide, is largely responsible for the rotten-egg smell that people often notice when they are close to a landfill. Methane, another landfill gas, is far more plentiful than hydrogen sulfide. According to the EPA, landfills are among the largest sources of methane in the United States, comprising an estimated 34 percent of all methane that is produced. The gas is highly flammable, and if it is not carefully piped out of landfills, it can result in a deadly explosion.

But if methane gas is captured and handled properly, it can be used as a source of energy. One city that is taking advantage of this technology is Seattle, Washington. Each year about 400,000 tons (362,874 metric tons) of garbage are shipped by rail from Seattle to a landfill in Arlington, Oregon. The methane is piped to a separate plant, where it powers combustion engines that generate electricity, which is then sold back to Seattle.

Although many other landfills capture and use methane, to do so requires a significant financial investment in technology. So most landfill owners just burn off the gas in a practice known as flaring. This sends the methane into the atmosphere, and because it is a powerful heat-trapping gas (along with carbon dioxide), many scientists say methane is a major contributor to global warming. As a January 2010 article in *Environment News Service* explains: "Methane, a primary component of landfill gas, is a greenhouse gas with more than 20 times the global warming potential of carbon dioxide. Using landfill gas as an energy resource prevents greenhouse gas emissions and reduces landfill odors."[14]

> " Although many other landfills capture and use methane, to do so requires a significant financial investment in technology. So most landfill owners just burn off the gas in a practice known as flaring. "

Incineration Concerns and Benefits

As garbage production continues to increase and landfill space grows scarcer, countries throughout the world are searching for better ways to dispose of waste. One solution that is becoming increasingly popular is burning garbage in incinerators, rather than dumping it into landfills, which saves a vast amount of disposal space. This is a controversial practice, though, because incinerators have long been notorious polluters, spewing deadly toxins into the atmosphere. Environmental groups cite this as a reason why burning is the wrong answer for the world's garbage problems. They often reference China and other developing countries, where outdated incineration plants contribute to serious air, soil, and water pollution.

Yet many of today's high-tech incinerators burn much cleaner than older models and are outfitted with devices that control toxic emissions. Journalist Elisabeth Rosenthal describes such a plant in an April 2010 article in the *New York Times*: "Dozens of filters catch pollutants, from mercury to dioxin, that would have emerged from its smokestack only a decade ago."[15]

Rosenthal was specifically referring to waste-to-energy plants, which burn garbage to produce electricity and fuel. Nearly 90 of these plants are operating in cities throughout the United States, but they are much more widespread in Europe, especially in Denmark, Germany, and the Netherlands. Denmark alone has 29 waste-to-energy plants, with 10 more under construction or in the planning phase. One that is located in the city of Horsholm is outfitted with dozens of devices that catch and filter out pollutants, cut carbon dioxide emissions, and, as Rosenthal writes, operate "so cleanly that many times more dioxin is now released from home fireplaces and backyard barbecues than from incineration."[16]

Pervasive Plastic Pollution

Of all the types of garbage that exist, plastic poses one of the most formidable environmental challenges—and its use and disposal continue to grow at a rapid rate. Plastic is used to make bottles for water, soda, and milk, as well as cleaning products, detergents, and beauty items. Containers for foods such as cottage cheese, sour cream, peanut butter, and yogurt are made of plastic, as are numerous other product packages. Although many of these items are recyclable, most plastic ends up in landfills. According to the EPA, an estimated 30.05 million tons (27.26 million metric tons) of plastic waste was generated in the United States in 2008, and only 7.1 percent was recovered for recycling. For such a vast amount of plastic to be thrown away is a serious problem because it does not biodegrade like many other types of garbage. Thus, as more and more plastic is dumped into landfills, it piles up and consumes valuable space.

> " Of all the types of garbage that exist, plastic poses one of the most formidable environmental challenges— and its use and disposal continue to grow at a rapid rate. "

One major problem with plastic waste is the proliferation of plastic grocery bags. According to the Worldwatch Institute, factories worldwide manufacture more than 4 trillion of the bags each year. Many thousands of those bags fly out of trash cans or off the backs of garbage trucks and drift along in the wind. They litter the countryside and get caught in fences, trees, and utility poles, as well as clog gutters, sewers, and waterways. Countries all over the world are plagued with litter from these bags. An August 2009 *Guardian* article describes South Africa's struggles with them: "Massing in their millions, crucified and shredded on barbed wire fences, plastic bags have come to be dubbed 'roadside daisies' in South Africa. Some now even mournfully refer to them as the country's national flower."[17]

Although plastic bags are a nuisance for humans, when they end up in the ocean they can be deadly for marine animals. A 2007 Worldwatch report states that these bags represent the major source of garbage in the ocean, especially near coastlines. Seabirds become entangled in plastic bags and drown because they cannot fly. Tens of thousands of seals, whales, and other marine animals die each year, either because the bags suffocate them or they starve after mistaking the bags for food and eating them. One creature that is threatened with extinction by plastic bags is the leatherback turtle, which is among the most ancient reptiles on earth. Floating on the ocean's surface the bags resemble jellyfish, the turtles' preferred food. The creatures eat the bags, and the plastic clogs their intestines, robbing them of vital nutrients and often causing starvation.

An Ongoing Challenge

From food scraps and yard waste to Styrofoam cups, plastic shopping bags, and billions of plastic water bottles, garbage poses numerous problems. With the global population continuing to escalate, and people throughout the world disposing of astounding volumes of trash, these problems grow more challenging every year. In the future, as more and more waste clogs landfills and ocean pollution continues to threaten marine life, solutions will be crucial in order to drastically reduce the amount of garbage that is generated and improve methods of disposal.

How Serious a Problem Is Garbage?

66 Lined municipal solid waste (MSW) landfills, like their open dump predecessors, are a failed technology for handling the discards of our society. Burying unsorted garbage in these facilities takes an unacceptable toll on public health, safety, and our environment.99

—Sierra Club Zero Waste Committee, "Zero Waste Cradle-to-Cradle Principles for the 21st Century: Municipal Solid Waste Landfills," September 2009. www.sierraclubmass.org

The Sierra Club is one of the most influential environmental organizations in the United States.

66 Landfills are no longer a threat to the environment or public health.99

—Floy Lilley, "Three Myths About Trash," Ludwig von Mises Institute, December 2, 2009. http://mises.org.

Lilley is an adjunct scholar at the Mises Institute, a libertarian organization that opposes government intervention in people's lives.

Bracketed quotes indicate conflicting positions.

* Editor's Note: While the definition of a primary source can be narrowly or broadly defined, for the purposes of Compact Research, a primary source consists of: 1) results of original research presented by an organization or researcher; 2) eyewitness accounts of events, personal experience, or work experience; 3) first-person editorials offering pundits' opinions; 4) government officials presenting political plans and/or policies; 5) representatives of organizations presenting testimony or policy.

66 More consumer items are being made now than ever before in the history of the planet. Many of them have an incredibly short life and are quickly discarded into the global garbage can. 99

—Nicky Scott, *Reduce, Reuse, Recycle*. White River Junction, VT: Chelsea Green, 2007.

Scott is an author from the United Kingdom who writes about recycling and composting issues.

66 Ninety percent of all rubbish floating in the world's oceans is plastic. In 2006, UN environment programs estimated that every square mile of ocean contained at least 46,000 pieces of floating plastic. 99

—Environmental Graffiti, "The North Pacific Gyre: 100 Million Tons of Garbage and Growing," August 18, 2009. www.environmentalgraffiti.com.

Environmental Graffiti is a Web site that features news articles about the environment.

66 In most countries throughout the developed world, organic waste is buried in landfill sites, where it decomposes into toxic effluent and methane, a greenhouse gas twenty-one times more potent than carbon dioxide. 99

—Tristram Stuart, *Waste: Uncovering the Global Food Scandal*. New York: Norton, 2009.

Stuart is an environmental author from the United Kingdom.

"More than 1 billion plastic water bottles end up in . . . California's trash each year, taking up valuable landfill space, leaking toxic additives, such as phthalates, into the groundwater and taking 1,000 years to biodegrade."

—Jared Blumenfeld and Susan Leal, "The Real Cost of Bottled Water," *San Francisco Chronicle,* February 18, 2007. http://articles.sfgate.com.

Blumenfeld is director of the San Francisco Department of the Environment, and Leal is general manager of the San Francisco Public Utilities Commission.

"70 percent of what Americans drink comes in a container, and bottled water has the lightest environmental footprint of them all."

—Brian Flaherty, "Testimony by Nestlé Waters North America on Pending Recycling Legislation in Connecticut," news release, Nestlé Waters North America, February 2, 2009. www.press.nestle-watersna.com.

Flaherty is Nestlé's director of public affairs.

"Marine and other aquatic litter (or debris) is . . . one of the world's most pervasive pollution problems impacting the shorelines, coastal waters, estuaries, and oceans, affecting the health of the seas and waterways."

—Ljubomir Jeftic, Seba Sheavly, and Ellik Adler, *Marine Litter: A Global Challenge,* April 2009. www.unep.org.

Jeftic, Sheavly, and Adler are specialists in marine biology.

❝Unpleasant odors can lower the quality of life for people who live near landfills and reduce local property values.❞

—U.S. Environmental Protection Agency, "Public Health, Safety, and the Environment," January 7, 2010. www.epa.gov.

The Environmental Protection Agency's mission is to protect human health and the environment.

❝One common misconception about landfills is that they have a negative effect on property values.❞

—National Solid Wastes Management Association, "Landfills," 2010. www.environmentalistseveryday.org.

The National Solid Wastes Management Association is a trade association representing North American companies that provide waste collection, recycling, and disposal services.

Facts and Illustrations

How Serious a Problem Is Garbage?

- According to the National Solid Wastes Management Association, the total volume of solid waste produced in the United States each year is equal to the weight of **2.3 million jumbo jets or 247,000 space shuttles.**

- The World Bank states that China's annual garbage generation is expected to reach **533 million tons** (483.53 million metric tons) by the year 2030.

- According to the Aluminum Association, more than **1 million tons** (907,185 metric tons) of aluminum containers and packaging are thrown away each year.

- If garbage generation in Britain continues to increase as it has in recent years, all of the country's landfills are expected to be **filled to capacity before 2020**.

- According to the National Recycling Coalition, Americans throw away enough office and writing paper each year to build a **wall 12 feet (3.66m) high that would stretch from New York to Seattle.**

- During an international coastal cleanup in September 2009, nearly 500,000 volunteers from 108 countries collected **7.4 million pounds** (3.36 million kg) of garbage.

- A report by the group Use Less Stuff states that between Thanksgiving and New Years' Day, Americans generate **6 million tons** (5.4 million metric tons) more waste than during the rest of the year.

- The Clean Air Council states that Americans throw away enough paper and plastic cups, forks, and spoons each year to circle the **equator 300 times**.

- According to the U.S. Department of Agriculture, Americans throw away an estimated 25 percent of food purchased—**52 billion pounds** (23.59 billion kg) each year.

- The Clean Air Council states that every year, Americans fill enough garbage trucks to form a line that would stretch from the **earth halfway to the moon**.

A Steady Rise in Trash

Since 1960 the amount of garbage generated in the United States has increased nearly 200 percent.

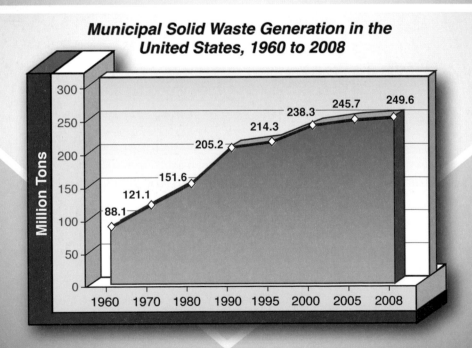

Municipal Solid Waste Generation in the United States, 1960 to 2008

Sources: Environmental Protection Agency, "Wastes: Text Version of Municipal Solid Waste Charts," November 17, 2009. www.epa.gov; Environmental Protection Agency, *Municipal Solid Waste in the United States: 2005 Facts and Figures*, October 2006.

Paper Is Biggest Source of Waste

The Environmental Protection Agency keeps track of garbage that is generated each year in the United States, including the quantity and type. At nearly one-third of the total, paper is the biggest source of waste.

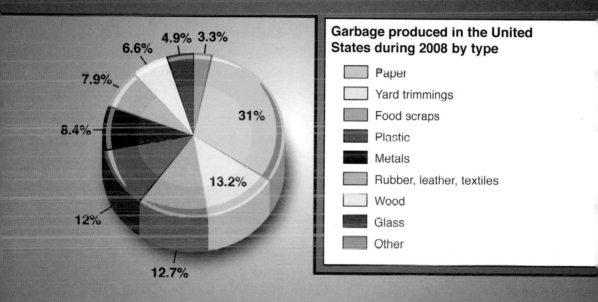

Garbage produced in the United States during 2008 by type

- Paper
- Yard trimmings
- Food scraps
- Plastic
- Metals
- Rubber, leather, textiles
- Wood
- Glass
- Other

Source: Environmental Protection Agency, "Wastes: Text Version of Municipal Solid Waste Charts," November 17, 2009. www.epa.gov.

- According to the U.S. Environmental Protection Agency, since 1977 the weight of 2-liter plastic soft drink bottles has been reduced from 2.4 ounces (68 grams) each to 1.8 ounces (51 grams), which has kept **250 million pounds** (113.4 million kg) of plastic per year out of the waste stream.

- As of 2008 Italy, Spain, Greece, and Britain were dumping more than **60 percent** of their garbage in landfills.

America's Largest Landfills

Waste management experts say that there is enough disposal capacity left in America's landfills to last for about 20 years. Some states, however, have little or no capacity left and must transport their garbage to landfills in other states. This graph shows the country's 10 largest landfills as of 2008.

Largest Landfills by Tons of Garbage Received—2008

Landfill	Tons
Apex Regional - Las Vegas, NV	3,199,653
Puente Hills - Whittier, CA	3,149,906
Newton County Landfill Partnership - Brock, IN	2,926,489
Okeechobee - Okeechobee, FL	2,640,000
Atlantic Waste - Waverly, VA	2,318,471
Rumpke Sanitary - Colerain Township, OH	2,174,660
Pine Tree Acres - Lenox, MI	2,142,348
El Sobrante - Corona, CA	2,104,362
Veolia Orchard Hills - Davis Junction, IL	2,084,445
Denver Arapahoe Disposal Site - Aurora, CO	1,946,126

Source: *Waste & Recycling News*, "Largest Landfills," November 9, 2009. www.wasterecyclingnews.com.

Is Toxic Garbage a Serious Problem?

❝That little old can of paint, paint thinner or finish, that bottle of insecticide, weed killer or oven cleaner, may contain toxins such as benzene, xylene, nervous-system damaging organophosphates and lye.❞

—Mother Nature Network, an online environmental news and information Web site.

❝Electronic wastes contain toxic substances such as lead, mercury, cadmium, and lithium. These toxic materials can be released upon disposal, posing a threat to human health and the environment.❞

—Tim Lindsey, associate director of the Illinois Sustainable Technology Center's Technical Assistance Program.

The town of Guiyu, located in the southern Chinese province of Guangdong, was once a peaceful rice farming community. Mei-sheng Chen has lived there for almost 30 years, and she has many fond memories, as described in an April 2008 article in the MyShantou Web site: "Every day, farmers furrowed fields with water buffalos, and fed their chickens and ducks in front of their houses. When night fell, the aroma of rice and fish wafted through town. There were two wells in the town, and all the residents gathered . . . their water at them. Water there was sweet and clean."[18] Chen's pleasant recollection of Guiyu is now a thing of the past. Although a few rice plants still dot the countryside, the town is now known as the electronic waste capital of China—and it is one of the most polluted places in the world.

Every day, ships carrying e-waste from the United States, Australia, Japan, and other industrialized countries arrive at the seaports of Hong

35

Kong and Nanhai, and huge truckloads of the waste are transported to Guiyu. Nearly everywhere one looks, there are enormous heaps of old computers, monitors, keyboards, printers, photocopiers, microwave ovens, DVD players, and televisions. In shops and open yards, workers use small tools, rocks, or their bare hands to crack open the e-waste and strip every piece of it down to its smallest components. They pull wires apart to remove copper, and "cook" circuit boards in big shallow pans over coal fires to recover the lead solder inside, which can then be sold. Some workers swirl computer chips in vats filled with hydrochloric acid and nitric acid to retrieve tiny bits of gold, platinum, and other valuable metals. After all the work has been completed and nothing more can be salvaged, scrap materials are heaped into enormous piles and set on fire. The blaze fills the air with the stench of burning plastic, rubber, and paint.

> " Every day, ships carrying e-waste from the United States, Australia, Japan, and other industrialized countries arrive at the seaports of Hong Kong and Nanhai, and huge truckloads of the waste are transported to Guiyu. "

The work that is performed in Guiyu is difficult and tedious, and workers toil for an average of 16 hours each day. Most are thankful because they have jobs they would not have had otherwise—but the town's primitive recycling practices have taken a heavy toll on the environment and human health. The water described by Chen as "sweet and clean" is now polluted and filthy, laced with high levels of acid and lead. The air is filled day and night with toxic smoke, and respiratory illness is rampant among adults and children. Reports by a Chinese university have shown that the town has the highest level of cancer-causing dioxins in the world, and an extraordinarily high rate of miscarriages. Another study showed that children in Guiyu have lead levels in their blood that are at least 50 percent higher than what is considered safe. According to Jim Puckett, who founded the e-waste watchdog group Basel Action Network, what is happening in Guiyu is nothing short of an environmental travesty. "You see women sitting by the fireplace burning laptop adapters, with rivers of ash pouring out of houses," he says. "We're dumping on the rest of the world."[19]

High-Tech Garbage

E-waste is an inevitable by-product of the modern electronic age, and it is the fastest-growing type of garbage worldwide. Today, "newer is better" is the prevailing philosophy, meaning that when fancier computers and other electronic gadgets become available, people are eager to buy them. In the United States alone, more than 205 million computers and computer-related products, and over 140 million cell phones are thrown away each year, and most of this e-waste ends up in landfills. A November 2009 report by the EPA states that more than 2.7 million tons (2.45 million metric tons) of consumer electronic equipment was disposed of during 2008, and only 13.6 percent was recycled. Thus, landfills were the dumping grounds for 2.3 million tons (2.09 million metric tons) of e-waste.

E-waste contains numerous toxic chemicals and heavy metals such as lead, cadmium, and mercury, and these toxins are not hazardous as long as electronic equipment remains intact. In landfills, however, e-waste is compacted and crushed, which causes the poisonous substances to leak out—and according to the EPA, e-waste accounts for 70 percent of the toxic substances in landfills. When these toxins seep through landfill liners, they contaminate soil and groundwater. Allen Hershkowitz, who is a senior scientist with the Natural Resources Defense Council, explains the potential effects of these toxins on human health: "Lead, cadmium, mercury, chromium, polyvinyl chlorides. All of these materials have known toxicological effects that range from brain damage to kidney disease to mutations, cancers."[20]

Toxic Household Garbage

When people think about toxins in the environment, residential kitchens, basements, and garages are probably not uppermost in their minds. Yet common household products are a major contributor to toxic garbage. Trash cans are often the repository for old drain and oven cleaners; mold and mildew removers; insect and weed killers; paint, paint thinners, and paint removers; metal and wood polish; and various types of glue. The same is true of batteries, including the dry-cell type used in flashlights, remote controls, and toys; and button-cell batteries, which are used in watches and hearing aids. When these household products end up in landfills, the toxins contained within them pose a threat to the environment, as the Sierra Club explains:

> Mechanisms to protect water supplies from waste only postpone, and do not prevent, pollution. Landfills generate leachate, a toxic liquid mix of chemicals in the waste mass. All landfill liners leak leachate, even initially from pinholes in the manufacturing process. Eventually liners and leachate collection systems will fail, causing large-scale groundwater contamination that cannot be remediated.[21]

A relatively recent—and fast-growing—problem with household toxic garbage involves compact fluorescent lightbulbs, also known as CFLs. These bulbs use much less electricity than older incandescent bulbs, which means they save immense amounts of energy. According to governmental sources, if every home in the United States replaced just one lightbulb with a CFL, this would save enough energy to light more than 2.5 million American homes for a year. But as energy-efficient CFLs have become more prolific, a new problem has arisen: The bulbs contain mercury, and if not properly disposed of, they are hazardous to the environment and anyone who is exposed to the toxin. John Skinner, who is executive director of the Solid Waste Association of North America, explains: "The problem with the bulbs is that they'll break before they get to the landfill. They'll break in containers, or they'll break in a dumpster or they'll break in the trucks. Workers may be exposed to very high levels of mercury when that happens."[22]

> "A relatively recent—and fast-growing—problem with household toxic garbage involves compact fluorescent lightbulbs, also known as CFLs."

Medical Garbage

Waste that is generated by health-care facilities such as hospitals, clinics, physicians' offices, dental practices, blood banks, and veterinary clinics is among the most dangerous type of toxic garbage that exists. It is crucial that items such as blood-soaked bandages, needles, protective gloves, surgical instruments, and removed body organs be disposed of properly so they do not endanger human health. For years it was common practice for medical waste to be burned in incinerators, but environmental groups have been lobbying to end this practice. They say that emissions from such incineration plants are extremely deadly because they are a major source of mercury, acid gases, nitrogen oxides, lead, and cadmium in the atmosphere. The EPA adds that medical incinerator emissions are America's third-largest source of dioxins. The Boston Chemical Data Corporation concurs, stating: "Medical waste incinerators produce more dioxins than all paper mill boilers, industrial furnaces and boilers, cars and trucks, hazardous waste incinerators, and coal and oil burning power plants combined."[23]

> " Waste that is generated by health-care facilities such as hospitals, clinics, physicians' offices, dental practices, blood banks, and veterinary clinics is among the most dangerous type of toxic garbage that exists. "

To address this problem, legislation enacted in September 2009 requires that medical incineration plants make improvements that reduce their emissions of toxic substances by 393,000 pounds (178,262kg) per year. In addition, the new law eliminates a loophole that previously allowed medical waste incinerators to exceed emissions limits whenever they started up, shut down, or malfunctioned. Katie Renshaw, who is with the environmental law firm Earthjustice, shares her thoughts about this ruling: "Hospitals and medical centers should be at the forefront of efforts to protect public health. The new rules on toxic air pollution from medical waste incinerators will save lives."[24]

A Swirling Toxic Soup

In 1997 an oceanographer named Charles Moore and his crew were on their way back to California after participating in a sailing race. They cut through the North Pacific Subtropical Gyre, an area in the Pacific

Ocean that stretches from about 575 miles (925.37km) off the California coast, past the Hawaiian Islands, and nearly as far as Japan. In this vast expanse of ocean, the combination of very little wind combined with tropical high-pressure systems keeps the water constantly churning like a gigantic whirlpool. As their boat drew closer, Moore expected to see only pristine ocean—but what he saw instead was a swirling mass of plastic garbage that stretched in every direction as far as he could see. He later wrote about his reaction: "It seemed unbelievable, but I never found a clear spot. In the week it took to cross the subtropical high, no matter what time of day I looked, plastic debris was floating everywhere: bottles, bottle caps, wrappers, fragments."[25] Several months after his discovery, Moore discussed what he had seen with a fellow oceanographer who referred to the plastic-filled gyre as a "garbage patch." But to Moore, the word "patch" did not even begin to describe such a horrifying example of ocean pollution.

> "
> **Garbage patches in the earth's oceans kill seabirds, turtles, albatross, and other marine creatures that mistake the plastic particles for food and eat it, which can lead to deadly intestinal blockages and starvation.**
> "

In the years since Moore's discovery, he and other scientists have continued to study and monitor the garbage patch, which is thought to be enormous. Some have speculated that it is twice the size of Texas, while others have estimated it to be bigger than the continental United States. But since the garbage patch is invisible to satellites, it cannot be measured from space, and changing weather patterns cause it to move around from season to season. So it is impossible for anyone to accurately determine its exact size. What is known is that in addition to intact pieces of debris, the garbage patch is a whirling mass of confetti-like plastic bits that Moore refers to as "plastic soup." The trillions of minuscule pieces are the remnants of a process known as photo-biodegradation, whereby exposure to sunlight breaks plastic down into particles no bigger than a grain of rice. But unlike biodegradation, the plastic never goes away and is held captive in the gyre by the constantly churning water.

Researchers have long suspected that other garbage-filled gyres existed, and in 2010 another enormous garbage patch was identified—this time in the Atlantic Ocean. A team of scientists trawling the sea between Bermuda and Portugal's Azores Islands took samples of the water every 100 miles (161km). Each time the scientists pulled up the trawl, they found it filled with plastic. "We found the great Atlantic garbage patch," says scientist Anna Cummins. "It's shocking to see it firsthand."[26]

Garbage patches in the earth's oceans kill seabirds, turtles, albatross, and other marine creatures that mistake the plastic particles for food and eat it, which can lead to deadly intestinal blockages and starvation. Also, like tiny sponges, the plastic bits soak up toxic chemicals in the water such as hydrocarbons, PCBs, and DDT, which poison marine creatures that feed on the plastic. Some scientists are convinced that the garbage patch also poses risks to human health. After small fish and other marine life ingest the poisons, the toxic substances are passed along to larger fish that prey on smaller ocean creatures. As a result, the toxins work their way up the food chain and into the bloodstreams of humans who eat the fish. As marine scientist Marcus Eriksen explains: "What goes into the ocean goes into these animals and onto your dinner plate. It's that simple."[27]

A Tough Problem to Solve

From hazardous household products, medical waste, and toxic e-waste to plastic-filled gyres in the earth's oceans, toxic garbage is a critical issue that needs to be treated as a high priority. If the amount produced is not curtailed, and disposal methods are not adequate to protect the environment and human health, this garbage will undoubtedly become an even more serious problem in the future.

Is Toxic Garbage a Serious Problem?

"Improper disposal of household hazardous wastes can include pouring them down the drain, on the ground, into storm sewers, or in some cases putting them out with the trash. The dangers of such disposal methods might not be immediately obvious, but improper disposal of these wastes can pollute the environment and pose a threat to human health."

—U.S. Environmental Protection Agency, "Household Hazardous Waste," September 30, 2008. www.epa.gov.

The Environmental Protection Agency's mission is to protect human health and the environment.

"A hidden waste management time bomb is ticking away, and health and safety professionals should understand its full dimensions: the disposal of medical waste, including used syringes, needles, lancets, and other sharps."

—Burton J. Kunic, "Assessing the Hidden Problem of Medical Waste Disposal," *Occupational Health & Safety,* April 1, 2010. http://ohsonline.com.

Kunic is the chair of a firm that provides disposal solutions for medical and pharmaceutical waste generated by non-health-care facilities.

* Editor's Note: While the definition of a primary source can be narrowly or broadly defined, for the purposes of Compact Research, a primary source consists of: 1) results of original research presented by an organization or researcher; 2) eyewitness accounts of events, personal experience, or work experience; 3) first-person editorials offering pundits' opinions; 4) government officials presenting political plans and/or policies; 5) representatives of organizations presenting testimony or policy.

Primary Source Quotes

"Vast quantities of solid and chemical waste from human activities are continually dumped and leach into the oceans, including plastics, sewage, sediment, oil and toxins that accumulate in food webs."

—Save Our Seas Foundation, "The Five Threats to Oceans and What You Can Do," Save Our Seas blog, 2009. www.saveourseas.com.

Headquartered in Geneva, Switzerland, the Save Our Seas Foundation implements and supports programs that protect earth's marine environment.

"Disposal or recycling of electronics can have significant human health and environmental impacts. Electronics can contain lead, brominated flame retardants, cadmium, mercury, arsenic and a wide range of other metals and chemical compounds."

—Valerie Thomas, "Electronic Waste: Investing in Research and Innovation to Reduce, Reuse and Recycle," testimony before the Committee on Science and Technology, U.S. House of Representatives, February 11, 2009. www.isye.gatech.edu.

Thomas is an associate professor of natural systems at the Georgia Institute of Technology in Atlanta.

"When we compromise the ocean's health, we compromise our own. Marine debris also directly impacts human health. Sharp items like broken glass or metal cans cut beachgoers, while disposable diapers, condoms, and old chemical drums introduce bacteria, toxic compounds, and other contaminants into the water."

—Ocean Conservancy, *Trash Travels,* April 13, 2010. www.oceanconservancy.org.

Ocean Conservancy is a nonprofit organization that works to protect the ocean and marine life.

66 **Even in regions such as the European Union, where disposal of hazardous waste is subject to stricter regulation, there is no precise information on what happens to as much as 75 percent of e-waste.** 99

—Greenpeace, "Fate of Vast Hazardous Electronics Waste Stream Unknown," February 21, 2008. www.greenpeace.org.

Greenpeace is an activist organization that works to expose environmental problems throughout the world and advocates practices that help solve them.

66 **Shipments of hazardous materials frequently move through populated or sensitive areas where an accident could result in loss of life, serious injury, or significant environmental damage.** 99

—Cynthia Douglass, speech before the Dangerous Goods Advisory Council at the 31st Annual Conference & Hazardous Materials Transportation Expo, November 19, 2009. www.phmsa.dot.gov.

Douglass is acting deputy administrator of the U.S. Department of Transportation's Pipeline & Hazardous Materials Safety Administration.

66 **The toxic materials contained in older electronic products that will hit the waste stream in the next 10 years are a potentially serious environmental problem. Effective ways of managing these legacy products remain an unresolved challenge.** 99

—Paul T. Anastas, "Hearing on E-Waste R&D Act," testimony before the U.S. House of Representatives Committee on Science and Technology, February 9, 2009. http://democrats.science.house.gov.

Anastas is with the Center for Green Chemistry and Green Engineering at Yale University.

66 Some exported used electronics are handled responsibly in countries with effective regulatory controls and by companies with advanced technologies, but a substantial quantity ends up in countries where disposal practices are unsafe to workers and dangerous to the environment. 99

—U.S. Government Accountability Office, *Electronic Waste: EPA Needs to Better Control Harmful U.S. Exports Through Stronger Enforcement and More Comprehensive Regulation*, August 2008. www.gao.gov.

Known as the "congressional watchdog," the Government Accountability Office works to improve the performance and accountability of the federal government for the benefit of the American people.

Is Toxic Garbage a Serious Problem?

- Worldwatch states that plastic pellets, which are used by the plastics industry to make products and are unintentionally released into oceans, can contain concentrated toxins up to **1 million times higher** than what is normally found in seawater.

- An October 2008 report in the publication *India West* states that the United States disposes of more than **150,000 tons** (136,078 metric tons) of electronic waste in India every year.

- People who change their own oil and dispose of it improperly dump the equivalent of **16 massive oil spills** into America's sewers and landfills every year.

- In an international coastal cleanup during September 2009, volunteers found **58,881 bottles of used oil/lube**, which is the amount that would be used to change the oil in nearly 12,000 mid-sized cars.

- The Oregon Department of Environmental Quality states that each American home contains from **3 to 8 gallons** (11.36 to 30.28L) of hazardous materials such as pesticides, herbicides, poisons, corrosives, solvents, fuels, paints, motor oil, antifreeze, and mercury and mercury-containing wastes.

- The U.S. Environmental Protection Agency estimates that **electronic waste** is growing two to three times faster than any other type of waste in the United States.

- Approximately **70 percent** of the world's e-waste ends up in Guiyu, China, and the World Health Organization states that the city's river water contains 2,400 times more lead than normal.

- According to an April 2010 article in the *Occupational Health & Safety* Web site, more than **3 billion syringes** are discarded in the regular trash each year by non-health-care industries such as home care, hospitality, and cleaning services.

States with E-Waste Legislation

Because the safe disposal of e-waste is a growing problem, a number of states have passed legislation that makes it mandatory for electronic equipment to be recycled. This map shows which states have passed such laws, and others that are considering them.

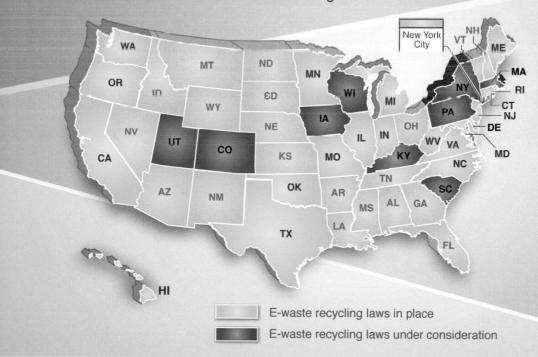

E-waste recycling laws in place

E-waste recycling laws under consideration

Source: Environmental Protection, "Indiana Passes First E-Waste Recycling Law in 2009," May 19, 2009.
http://eponline.com.

Electronic Trash Threatens Health and Environment

Discarded electronic devices such as computers and cell phones contain many components that are potentially hazardous to human health and the environment. When these devices end up in landfills or with recyclers who do not follow proper handling procedures, the effects can be serious and long-lasting.

Computer/ E-Waste Component	Potential Health Hazard
Cathode ray tubes (CRTs)	• Silicosis • Cuts from CRT glass in case of implosion • Inhalation or contact with phosphor containing cadmium or other metals
Printed circuit boards	• Tin and lead inhalation • Possible brominated dioxins, beryllium, cadmium, mercury inhalation
Dismantled printed circuit board processing	• Toxicity to workers and nearby residents from tin, lead, brominated dioxins, beryllium, cadmium, and mercury inhalation • Respiratory irritation
Chips and other gold-plated components	• Acid contact with eyes, skin may result in • permanent injury • Inhalation of mists and fumes of acids, chlorine and sulphur dioxide gases can cause respiratory irritation to severe effects including pulmonary edema, circulatory failure, and death
Plastics from computers and peripherals, e.g. printers, keyboards, etc.	• Probable hydrocarbon, brominated dioxin, and heavy metal exposures
Computer wires	• Brominated and chlorinated dioxins, polycyclic aromatic hydrocarbons (PAH) (carcinogenic) exposure to workers living in the burning works area
Miscellaneous computer parts encased in rubber or plastic, such as steel rollers	• Hydrocarbon including PAH, and potential dioxin exposure
Toner cartridges	• Respiratory tract irritation • Carbon black possible human carcinogen • Cyan, yellow, and magenta toners unknown toxicity
Secondary steel or copper and precious metal smelting	• Exposure to dioxins and heavy metals

Potential Environmental Hazard
• Lead, barium, and other heavy metals leaching into groundwater, release of toxic phosphor
• Air emission of same substances
• Tin and lead contamination of immediate environment including surface and groundwater. * Brominated dioxins, beryllium, cadmium, and mercury emissions
• Hydrocarbons, heavy metals, brominated substances, etc., discharged directly into rivers and banks • Acidifies the river destroying fish and flora
• Emissions of brominated dioxins and heavy metals, and hydrocarbons
• Hydrocarbon ashes including PAHs discharged into air, water, and soil
• Hydrocarbon ashes including PAHs discharged into air, water, and soil
• Cyan, yellow, and magenta toners unknown toxicity
• Emissions to dioxins and heavy metals

Source: The Basel Action Network and Silicon Valley Toxins Coalition, "Exporting Harm: The Hi-Tech Trashing of Asia," February 25, 2002.

- Each year, the European Union throws away **1.4 billion** tons (1.3 billion metric tons) of garbage, of which an estimated 44 million tons (40 million metric tons) is toxic.

- According to the environmental site Mother Nature Network, mothballs qualify as toxic garbage because they give off fumes of either dichlorobenzene, a **chemical that attacks the nervous system**, or naphthalene, which can produce nausea, jaundice, and liver and kidney damage.

- The single **largest source of mercury** in household garbage is batteries, especially alkaline and small batteries, which are used to power watches, hearing aids, and other small electronic items.

- After the state of Washington passed legislation mandating that electronics manufacturers cover consumers' recycling costs, **38 million pounds** (17.24 million kg) of e-waste was kept out of landfills in one year alone.

How Effective Is Recycling?

66 Recycling has environmental benefits at every stage in the life cycle of a consumer product—from the raw material with which it's made to its final method of [disposal].99

—U.S. Environmental Protection Agency, whose mission is to protect human health and the environment.

66 We've had it drilled into us that recycling is an environmental virtue—and it is a good step to take, as a last resort. But it's almost always better to reduce or reuse rather than to recycle.99

—Sierra Club, a grassroots environmental organization that works to protect communities, wild places, and the planet itself.

When Mike and Tricia Barry decided to tear down a deteriorating bungalow and have a new home built on its large, tree-shaded lot, they cringed at the thought of all the waste that would be generated. Being environmentally conscious and avid supporters of recycling, they rejected the notion of having the house demolished, with potentially usable materials destroyed and dumped in a landfill. Instead, they opted to have it deconstructed, or carefully dismantled—and in the process, the California couple was hailed for achieving a true recycling success story.

Mike Barry made arrangements to donate all salvageable materials, then he hired a licensed firm to handle the deconstruction. The home's double-pane windows were sturdy and perfectly suitable for reuse, and appliances were relatively new and in excellent condition. Wood from the frame was dismantled and stacked on pallets, and damaged wood was

51

ground in a chipper to be used as landscaping mulch or for production of particleboard. Flooring, roofing, heating vents, doors, and copper plumbing were all carefully removed, as were bricks from the home's exterior. Even nails were salvaged after an enormous magnet pulled them out one by one. By the time the project was complete, an estimated 80 to 85 percent of the Barrys' house had been recycled, with reusable materials delivered to Habitat for Humanity and other organizations that would put them to good use. All that was thrown away was asbestos-laden drywall and stucco that had been on the outside of the home—so little waste that it fit in just one large metal trash bin. "We basically had it deconstructed piece by piece," says Mike Barry. "Mainly, the difference is we didn't tear it down and throw it all into a landfill." He and his wife feel good about the decision they made, and wish more people would do the same. He explains: "I don't see how anyone cannot do it. It also says something positive to our children."[28]

More Trash, More Recycling

Over the years, the volume of garbage produced in the United States has substantially increased, but recycling has grown as well. According to the EPA, an estimated 61 million tons (55 million metric tons) of paper, aluminum, steel, glass, plastic, packaging, and wood waste was recycled during 2008. Another 22 million tons (20 million metric tons) of food and yard waste was recycled into compost. Together, these efforts kept millions of tons of reusable material out of landfills. And while the average total of recycled waste was only 33.2 percent, that is more than triple the 1980 recycling rate and over 5 times higher than the rate in the 1960s. As the Natural Resources Defense Council explains: "The United States now recycles one third of its municipal waste—trash we generate in our homes, schools and non-industrial businesses—compared to just 6 percent in 1960." The council adds that the amount of

> **Over the years, the volume of garbage produced in the United States has substantially increased, but recycling has grown as well.**

material recycled today "equals the total quantity of garbage the United States produced in 1960."[29] Throughout the country, growing numbers of cities and towns have implemented recycling programs, and this has led to a significant decrease in the garbage that is sent to landfills. The EPA reports that landfill disposal has decreased from 89 percent of total waste generated in 1980 to 54 percent in 2008.

Turning Old into New

As recycling efforts have continued to expand, more and more products are being manufactured from recycled materials. According to Chaz Miller, who is program director for the Environmental Industry Associations, recycled products are the same quality as those made from scratch. He explains: "In fact, most products made from recyclables can't be distinguished from products that aren't. Products that are made from used aluminum, steel, glass, plastic or paper

> And while the average total of recycled waste was only 33.2 percent, that is more than triple the 1980 recycling rate and over 5 times higher than the rate in the 1960s.

must meet the same manufacturing specifications as they did when they were made from virgin raw materials. When it comes to quality, recycled products are as good as new!"[30]

The variety of products that can be made from recycled materials is not only extensive; it is also diverse. Glass bottles and jars can become new glass containers, but they can also be used to make insulation and other construction materials. Old tires can be recycled into asphalt for road surfaces and to make rubber mulch for playgrounds. Plastic bottles are made into packaging containers, sleeping bag insulation, carpet backing, tool handles, and auto parts, as well as clothing. A company called Wellman uses recycled plastic soda and water bottles to manufacture a fleece fiber known as Eco-fi (formerly EcoSpun). The fabric is used to make vests, jackets, pants, blanket throws, and accessories, as well as carpets and home furnishings.

Paper, which is recycled more than any other material, is also versatile for making new products. According to the EPA, nearly 37 percent of the fiber used to make new paper products was derived from recycled sources during 2007. In addition to common products such as stationery and cardboard packages, paper is used to make thousands of other items. These include masking tape, bandages, lamp shades, animal bedding, and egg cartons, as well as paper money, car insulation, coffee filters, and hospital gowns. Paper's only limitation is that, unlike glass and aluminum, both of which can be recycled indefinitely, its recycling life is limited. Each time it is recycled, the fibers get shorter and the quality decreases, so either more virgin fiber will need to be added or the paper will need to be disposed of.

> **The variety of products that can be made from recycled materials is not only extensive; it is also diverse.**

Saving Energy and Natural Resources

A number of studies have shown that manufacturing products from recycled items rather than virgin materials saves energy. According to the EPA, the savings achieved during 2008 by recycling and composting 83 million tons (75 million metric tons) of waste amounted to 1.3 quadrillion Btu of energy, which is the equivalent of more than 10.2 billion gallons (38.61 billion L) of gasoline. As Miller writes:

> Life cycle studies show that recycling usually has less impact on the environment and requires less energy than making products out of virgin materials. This is because the environmental and energy impact of extracting virgin materials from the soil or from forests, transforming them into raw materials and then turning them into an end product is greater than the environmental and energy impact of collecting those products, processing them and using them as raw materials to make new products.[31]

The Chicago Conservation Corps adds that manufacturing bottles from recycled plastic uses 70 percent less energy than creating them from new materials, and making 1 ton (0.9 metric ton) of paper from recycled fibers rather than virgin materials saves up to 31 trees and 7,000 gallons (25,498L) of water.

Aluminum cans are often touted as a shining example of how recycling saves energy. Recycling just 1 aluminum can saves enough energy to keep a 100-watt lightbulb burning for nearly 4 hours or to run a television for 3 hours. Referring to the recyclability of aluminum beverage cans as "recycling at its finest," Alcoa Recycling describes the benefits: "A recycled can requires 95 percent less energy, generates 95 percent less emissions and creates 97 percent less water pollution than generating new metal. Therefore, purchasing beverages in aluminum cans, then recycling is a simple way to reduce one's carbon footprint."[32] Alcoa adds that in 2008, aluminum cans reached a 54.2 percent recycling rate, which was the highest of any beverage container.

The Challenges of Recycling

Recycling has proved to be beneficial in many ways, but it is not without challenges. The biggest hurdle for many people is convenience: It is often easier to throw all garbage together in one bin than to spend time sorting glass, metal, paper, and different types of plastic. Also, certain types of materials are not recyclable, and if they get mixed in with recyclables that are being processed, the entire batch can be contaminated. Even people who want to recycle may be discouraged from doing so if their communities do not offer curbside pickup and recycling facilities are too far away.

> " Challenges are also faced by owners of recycling operations because the ability to sell their wares is dependent on the state of the economy. "

Another challenge posed by recycling is cost. Landfill disposal fees, known as tipping fees, are usually cheaper than what recycling operations charge. Because higher costs are passed along to consumers, they may refrain from recycling in order to save money. In Rapid City, South Dakota, the average cost to dump 1 ton (0.9 metric ton) of mixed waste is $53, compared with about $600 to $800 per ton for recyclable materials. But according to Jerry Wright, the city's solid waste manager, it is short-sighted to focus on that. He explains: "If you just look at what it costs to throw it in the hole and cover it up, yes, of course it is cheaper. If we were burying everything in the landfill, we'd be operating in the area of $20 a ton. But this landfill wouldn't last us long."[33] Building a new landfill in Rapid City would cost as much as $20 million, and Wright says that must be considered when evaluating whether recycling is worth the cost. He and other Rapid City officials view recycling as a priority because it helps to extend the life of the landfill as long as possible—which will save money in the long run.

Challenges are also faced by owners of recycling operations because the ability to sell their wares is dependent on the state of the economy. During today's tough economic times, the price that recyclers can get for recovered materials has dropped dramatically. As a March 2009 article in *U.S. News & World Report* explains: "Less consumer spending leads to less manufacturing, which cuts down on the need for goods, like cardboard for packaging, obtained from the recycling bin. A plunge in prices follows. Recyclers see profits drop—and may cut services."[34] Michael Benedetto, who owns TFC Recycling in Virginia, has struggled because of the bad economy. In the past Benedetto could sell aluminum cans for more than a dollar per pound, but as of March 2009 his price had been slashed in half. Other recyclers have seen paper and cardboard that sold for $200 per ton drop to just $20 per ton within a few months, and the same is true with plastic and glass. When prices fluctuate like this, some recycling operations are able to hang on until the economy improves and prices begin to rise again. Others, however, are driven out of business.

Mixed Success with E-Waste Recycling

As people are becoming more aware of threats to the environment from e-waste, many are opting to recycle their old computers and other electronic devices. Some major electronics manufacturers such as Hewlett-Packard, Dell, and Apple are committed to taking back their products and recycling them in a responsible way. In 1997 Hewlett-Packard became the first computer manufacturer to operate its own recycling facility, and in 2007 the company reached its goal of recycling more than 1 billion pounds (453.59 million kg) of products and materials.

Yet not all companies that claim to be electronics recyclers are legitimate—in fact, people often have no idea what sort of "recycling" is actually being done. These so-called recyclers have been caught illegally shipping e-waste to developing countries such as China and India, where the cost to recycle is a fraction of what it is in the United States. According to the environmental watchdog group Basel Action Network, an estimated 80 percent of the e-waste that consumers think is being recycled at facilities in the United States is actually shipped overseas.

Growing Potential

Although recycling is not the answer to all problems caused by the world's burgeoning garbage, many believe it is an important step. Recycling means less waste is dumped in landfills, which saves valuable space. Recycling results in significant energy savings, as well as preserving natural resources because when products are manufactured with recycled materials, fewer virgin materials are needed. In the coming years, if the challenges associated with recycling can be overcome, it will likely become even more of a benefit than it is today.

How Effective Is Recycling?

Primary Source Quotes

66 One ton of recycled paper uses: 64% less energy, 50% less water, 74% less air pollution, saves 17 trees and creates 5 times more jobs than one ton of paper products from virgin wood pulp.99

—CU Recycling, "Recycling Facts," 2008. http://recycling.colorado.edu.

Located at the University of Colorado at Boulder, CU Recycling is one of the leading campus recycling programs in the United States.

66 Manufacturing paper, glass, and plastic from recycled materials uses appreciably more energy and water, and produces as much or more air pollution, as manufacturing from raw materials does. Resources are not saved and the environment is not protected.99

—Floy Lilley, "The Economics of Recycling," Lew Rockwell.com, November 24, 2009. www.lewrockwell.com.

Lilley is an adjunct scholar at the Mises Institute, a libertarian organization that opposes government intervention in people's lives.

Bracketed quotes indicate conflicting positions.

* Editor's Note: While the definition of a primary source can be narrowly or broadly defined, for the purposes of Compact Research, a primary source consists of: 1) results of original research presented by an organization or researcher; 2) eyewitness accounts of events, personal experience, or work experience; 3) first-person editorials offering pundits' opinions; 4) government officials presenting political plans and/or policies; 5) representatives of organizations presenting testimony or policy.

"In virtually all recycling processes I've come to meet, the savings in energy consumption from elimination of the extraction and refinement far outweigh the costs of collection and processing."

—Tom Larsen, "Does Recycling Really Benefit the Planet or Save Energy?" GreenSmart Notebook, December 22, 2008. http://tomlarsen.typepad.com.

Larsen is the president of GreenSmart, a manufacturer of bags made from eco-conscious materials.

"Products are becoming more recyclable. New techniques allow for easy and quick disassembly. Companies are exploring the use of plastic resins that can be reused in new products. They are also working with recyclers to help understand how product design impacts the recycling process."

—Phillip J. Bond, "Electronic Waste: Investing in Research and Innovation and Fostering a Public-Private Partnership to Meet the Challenge," testimony before the U.S. House of Representatives Committee on Science and Technology, February 11, 2009. http://democrats.science.house.gov.

Bond is president of Tech America, a group that represents the U.S. technology industry.

"Today, recycling programs for electronics and other consumer products have low recycling rates both because collection programs are difficult for consumers to use and because the products are difficult to recycle."

—Valerie Thomas, "Electronic Waste: Investing in Research and Innovation to Reduce, Reuse and Recycle," testimony before the Committee on Science and Technology, U.S. House of Representatives, February 11, 2009. www.isye.gatech.edu.

Thomas is an associate professor of natural systems at the Georgia Institute of Technology in Atlanta.

❝We are currently witnessing a drastic drop in the market for traditional recyclables because of the downturn in our economy and the economies of global trading partners. Also, recycling and refabricating these materials often uses more energy than creating virgin products.❞

—Jeffrey E. Surma, "Finding a Sustainable Future at the Dump," *Boston Globe,* January 12, 2009. www.boston.com.

Surma is president and CEO of InEnTec, an Oregon-based firm specializing in the conversion of waste into clean, renewable products.

❝Over the last 20 years I have watched a widespread green consciousness emerge and sweep over our culture, and I believe that the recycling revolution had everything to do with that.❞

—Eric Lombardi, "MoJo Forum: Is Recycling a Waste?" *Mother Jones,* April 20, 2009. http://motherjones.com.

Lombardi is executive director of Eco-Cycle, one of the largest nonprofit recyclers in the United States.

❝In 1973, not a single curbside recycling program existed in the United States. Today, there are more than 8,000 in operation throughout the country.❞

—Natural Resources Defense Council, "The Past, Present and Future of Recycling," March 28, 2008. www.nrdc.org.

The Natural Resources Defense Council is an environmental action organization based in New York City.

❝Of the 170 million tons of municipal solid waste disposed [of] each year in the U.S., 24.3% is paper and paperboard. Reducing and recycling paper will decrease releases of numerous air and water pollutants to the environment, and will also conserve energy and forest resources, thereby reducing greenhouse gas emissions.❞

—Brenda Platt, David Ciplet, Kate M. Bailey, and Eric Lombardi, *Stop Trashing the Climate,* June 2008. www.stoptrashingtheclimate.com.

Platt is with the Institute for Local Self-Reliance, Ciplet is with the Global Anti-Incinerator Alliance, and Bailey and Lombardi are with Eco-Cycle.

How Effective Is Recycling?

- According to the U.S. Environmental Protection Agency, about **80 percent** of what Americans throw in the trash is recyclable, yet the recycling rate is only **33 percent**.

- The Environmental Defense Fund states that recycling glass instead of making it from virgin materials (silica) reduces mining waste by **70 percent**, water use by **50 percent**, and air pollution by **20 percent**.

- According to the California Department of Conservation, if all the **Sunday newspapers** printed in the United States were recycled, this would save **26 million trees per year**.

- The Steel Recycling Institute states that the energy saved by steel recycling is equal to the electrical power used by **18 million homes** each year.

- According to the Aluminum Association, recycling saves **95 percent** of the energy required to make aluminum from bauxite ore.

- The U.S. Environmental Protection Agency states that **8,660 curbside recycling programs** were in place in the United States during 2008, which was a decrease from 8,875 in 2002.

- The Aluminum Association reports that **52 percent** of the aluminum used in North America comes from domestically produced primary aluminum, **34 percent** is derived from recycled materials, and **14 percent** is imported.

- According to the U.S. Environmental Protection Agency, about **3,510 community composting programs** were operational in 2008, up from 3,227 in 2002.

- The environmental group Earth911 states that every ton (0.9 metric ton) of paper that is recycled saves more than **3.3 cubic yards** (2.52 cu. m) of landfill space.

Recycling Rates Vary Widely

Americans recycled or composted approximately one-third of the 250 million tons of trash generated in 2008. Certain items such as auto batteries had an extremely high rate of recycling while other items such as plastic bottles and jars had a much lower rate of recycling.

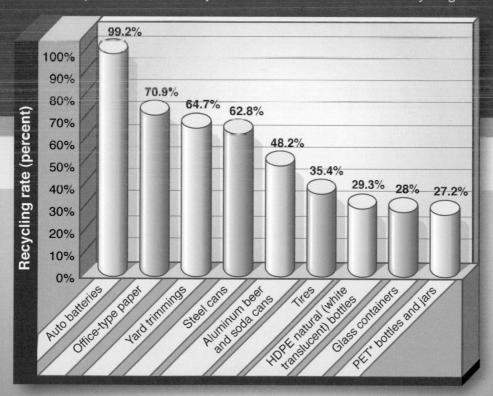

*PET stands for polyethylene terephthalate, a type of plastic used in bottles for soft drinks and water.

Source: Environmental Protection Agency, *Municipal Solid Waste Generation, Recycling, and Disposal in the United States: Facts and Figures for 2008*, November 2009. www.epa.gov.

Recycling in Major Cities

In March 2009 *Waste & Recycling News* published the results of a survey that examined America's most populous cities and their recycling rates, some of which are shown on this graph.

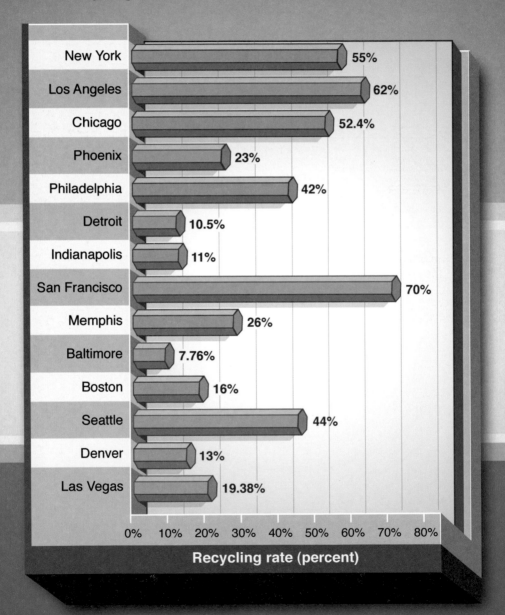

City	Recycling rate
New York	55%
Los Angeles	62%
Chicago	52.4%
Phoenix	23%
Philadelphia	42%
Detroit	10.5%
Indianapolis	11%
San Francisco	70%
Memphis	26%
Baltimore	7.76%
Boston	16%
Seattle	44%
Denver	13%
Las Vegas	19.38%

Recycling rate (percent)

Note: Starting at the top, cities are ranked from largest to smallest based on population.

Source: *Waste & Recycling News*, "Municipal Recycling Survey," March 2, 2009. www.wasterecyclingnews.com.

- By recycling more than **57,000 tons** (51,710 metric tons) of steel cans, the reduction in greenhouse gases is equivalent to taking more than **21,000 cars off the road** each year.

- More than **37 percent** of the fiber used to make new paper products in the United States comes from recycled sources.

Recyclable Materials

To encourage businesses and residents to cut down on the amount of trash that is taken to landfills, communities throughout the United States have implemented recycling programs. This table shows the wide variety of materials that are recyclable (although what recycling operations will accept varies from community to community).

Paper	Office paper, newspapers, magazines, catalogs, telephone books, junk mail, cardboard boxes
Glass	Beverage bottles, food jars
Aluminum	Beverage cans, foil, clean pie tins, aluminum siding, metal frames from lawn furniture
Steel	Food and beverage cans, empty aerosol cans, empty paint cans
Plastic	PET soda and water bottles, milk jugs, detergent bottles
Yard debris	Leaves, twigs, tree and bush trimmings, grass
Food waste	Fruit and vegetable trimmings, eggshells, coffee grounds with filters, teabags (no meats, dairy foods, fats/oils, bones)
Miscellaneous	Plastic bags, Styrofoam, used motor oil, batteries

Source: Pennsylvania Department of Environmental Protection, "What Can Be Recycled?" September 1, 2009. www.dep.state.pa.us.

How Can Garbage Be Reduced in the Future?

66 **Experts say that continuing to increase our recycling rates will help pull us out of the garbage heap and reduce global warming emissions. And that a necessary counterpart to that strategy is to cut down on the waste we produce in the first place.** 99

—Natural Resources Defense Council, which works to protect wildlife and wild places and to ensure a healthy environment for all life on the earth.

66 **Recycling provides a limited contribution to solving a problem that is more about consumption than about trash. But it reminds us of the threads that bind our individual households to the planet and the activities of our daily lives to its future.** 99

—Susan Strasser, a professor of history at the University of Delaware and the author of *Waste and Want: A Social History of Trash*.

In the early twentieth century, garbage reduction was not something that really concerned people. The population of the United States was only about one-third of what it is today, and the volume of garbage that was generated by Americans was extremely small. As a February 1919 article in *Popular Science Monthly* stated: "Definite figures can be worked out for the quantities and contents of garbage in spite of its variable character and amount. According to a report by the American Chemical Society, the average quantity per person is one half pound a day."[35] Even with so little garbage being produced, Americans were still encouraged to save and reuse materials such as paper, wool, rubber, cotton, leather, and metals. But unlike today, this conservation effort was not related to concerns about an overabundance of garbage, overflowing landfills, or potential damage to the environment. Rather, acute shortages during World War I prompted the U.S. government to adopt a "Don't waste waste—save it" philosophy in order to avoid such shortages in the future.

Over the following decades, scores of new materials and innovative products were introduced, which radically influenced Americans' perspectives about consumption. The country moved from a waste-conscious society to a throw-away society, one in which consumers increasingly coveted disposable items and demanded convenience—and as this happened, the volume of garbage rose dramatically. Since 1919, when each person in the United States generated 0.5 pounds (0.23kg) of garbage per day, the volume in 2008 had risen to 4.5 pounds (2.04kg) per person—an increase of nearly 222 million tons (201.4 million metric tons) of garbage *per year*. With such astounding growth in the amount of garbage, it is no wonder that waste management experts, environmental groups, and government officials are examining all possible options to significantly reduce the garbage that is produced now and in the future.

> **Since 1919, when each person in the United States generated 0.5 pounds (0.23kg) of garbage per year, the volume in 2008 had risen to 4.5 pounds (2.04kg) per person—an increase of nearly 222 million tons (201.4 million metric tons) of garbage *per year*.**

The First of the Three Rs

Although people do not always agree about how serious America's garbage problems are, few would argue that the most effective way to cut back on the volume of trash is to start at the beginning—using less materials up front to eliminate waste before it is produced. This is the meaning of the "reduce" part of the three Rs, which is also known as "precycling." The waste reduction group CalRecycle explains:

> An example of waste reduction is reducing unnecessary packaging from manufactured products and produce. If

this excess packaging could be avoided, no one would have to be concerned with the cost and effort of collecting the excess packaging, separating it for recycling, breaking it down, transporting it to manufacturers, and then integrating the recycled materials back into the manufacturing process.[36]

Some examples of reduced packaging include plastic milk bottles; food cans; cereal boxes; fruit juice cartons; and aluminum, glass, and plastic beverage containers, all of which are significantly lighter today than in the past.

A number of major companies have embraced the source reduction concept and have proved that it works. Dell Computer, for example, has implemented what it calls a global packaging reduction target for desktop computers and laptops. Dell's goal is to make a 10 percent reduction in packaging and shipping materials worldwide, which will eliminate 20 million pounds (9.1 million kg) of waste by 2012. Another company that is strongly committed to source reduction is the fast-food giant McDonald's. Its drinking straws were redesigned to be 20 percent lighter, which reduced McDonald's trash by an estimated 1 million pounds (453,592kg) per year.

Frito-Lay has an equally aggressive commitment to precycling. The company has made major adjustments, including reducing the amount of material used in packaging by 10 percent over the past 5 years. As its Web site states: "If that doesn't sound like much, consider that that's enough to cover more than 72,000 football fields. And, by improving our chip bags to extend their shelf life, we've saved 5 million pounds of packaging and product from going into landfills."[37] One way that Frito-Lay has changed its bags is by redesigning the packaging for Lay's and Ruffles potato chips. Company officials state that by switching from composite plastic bags to metalized plastic bags, the packages are now 25 percent lighter. This has kept more than 6 million pounds (2.72 million kg) of packaging material out of landfills each year. Another change that may sound small has achieved big results for Frito-Lay. Bag seals used on Frito's corn chips were reduced from 0.5 inch (1.27cm), which is the industry standard, to 0.25 inch (0.635cm). Company officials estimate that this change resulted in a 5 percent reduction in the Frito's packaging that ends up in landfills.

Procter & Gamble is another major corporation that has source reduction at the top of its priority list. With more than 300 product brands sold all over the world, the company uses most every packaging material available. Its staff scientists have experimented with a number of different methods to reduce packaging and have made significant progress. For instance, after switching one of P&G's beauty products from a solid plastic case to a combination of cardboard and plastic, the scientists found that content was reduced by 65 percent per package, resulting in 1.1 million pounds (498,952kg) less material per year.

From Trash to Treasure

Finding uses for older products is certainly not a new idea. Consignment shops that sell used merchandise have long been popular with thrift-conscious shoppers, and many people enjoy frequenting flea markets, estate sales, and auctions. But with growing awareness of the necessity to lessen the amount of waste that is produced, the word *reuse* has taken on a renewed meaning. Rather than throwing away old clothing, appliances, televisions, cell phones, toys, computers, or other items that may not be worth enough to sell, growing numbers of people now opt to donate these items to others who might be able to use them.

Groups such as Freecycle have played a pivotal role in building awareness of and enthusiasm for donating used items. According to its Web site, if the amount of merchandise given away in one year were stacked in garbage trucks, the weight would exceed 400 million pounds (181.44 million kg) and stand 5 times taller than Mount Everest. A January 2010 editorial in the *Waco Tribune* touts what Freecycle has accomplished: "It's kind of like pay it forward with no strings attached—just good feelings toward others in the

> " Rather than throwing away old clothing, appliances, televisions, cell phones, toys, computers, or other items that may not be worth enough to sell, growing numbers of people now opt to donate these items to others who might be able to use them. "

community." The editorial adds that in addition to helping people obtain items they need, Freecycle also benefits the planet because "every item spared from our overcrowded landfills is one less item polluting our lands."[38]

The concept of reuse is by no means limited to individual consumers. Corporations are also embracing it, in the same way that they have become committed to source reduction. Frito-Lay, for example, encourages its salespeople to return shipping cartons and has achieved a 99 percent return rate. The company reuses the cartons at least 5 or 6 times and estimates that this effort saves about 5 million trees per year.

Rethinking E-Waste

Because of the significant challenge posed by ever-increasing volumes of e-waste, many organizations are committed to doing their part to reduce it. A program created by eBay known as the Rethink Initiative is helping this growing effort, and its Web site sums up the focus: "It's no small issue. Hundreds of millions of retired computers, cell phones and electronics sit idle or are discarded by Americans every year. We need to make smart choices about what we do with these products to help ensure a clean environment for future generations."[39] Rethink Initiative partners include major corporations such as Intel, Apple, Dell, Gateway, Hewlett-Packard, IBM, and Nokia, as well as Best Buy, Goodwill Industries, the U.S. Postal Service, United Parcel Service (UPS), the U.S. Environmental Protection Agency, and the International Association of Electronics Recyclers.

> **The creators of the Rethink Initiative, as well as its partners, hope that their combined efforts will expand awareness of e-waste and help people make better choices about how to dispose of it.**

On the Rethink Initiative Web site, people can list used electronics they want to sell or give away, and if they need suggestions about where to donate, they can find that, too. For items that are beyond reuse or repair, the site offers a list of legitimate recyclers to help people make arrangements for recycling their old electronics.

The creators of the Rethink Initiative, as well as its partners, hope that their combined efforts will expand awareness of e-waste and help people make better choices about how to dispose of it. As eBay president and CEO Meg Whitman stated before leaving the company: "EBay's millions of users can be a powerful force for good. The Rethink Initiative will educate consumers on how to properly dispose of or recycle the millions of tons of e-waste they confront each year. We're extremely excited about the positive role eBay's user community will play in confronting this environmental dilemma."[40]

Making Garbage Count

Reduction, reuse, and recycling programs are making a significant difference in people's perspectives about garbage, as well as helping to cut down on the volume of waste. Waste will always be produced, so the challenge for scientists is to preserve landfill space as much as possible, and in the process find ways to make garbage useful. One area that is viewed as having excellent potential is technology that converts waste products into fuel, which is already being used in areas throughout California. According to a January 5, 2010, article in the *Seattle Times*, nearly 500 trucks that used to run on diesel fuel are now powered by gas that is produced from landfill trash. At the liquefied natural gas facility in Altamont, California, more than 100 wells suck methane gas from the landfill into black tubes. After being purified, the methane is converted into liquefied natural gas, and then pumped into garbage and recycling trucks at a fueling station in Oakland. The EPA's Tom Frankiewicz shares his thoughts about the advantages of this technology: "Methane is the second most important greenhouse gas after carbon dioxide. Methane is also the main component of natural gas, so by capturing and using methane as an energy source you get an even bigger bang for the buck."[41]

> In addition to making fuel, garbage can also be converted to electricity in a high-tech process known as plasma gasification.

In addition to making fuel, garbage can also be converted to electricity in a high-tech process known as plasma gasification. Waste is exposed to super-hot temperatures that vaporize it, creating a synthetic gas (known as syngas) that can be used to generate electrical power. According to the EPA, plasma gasification results in clean energy because no dioxins, mercury, or other toxins are emitted into the atmosphere.

Challenges Ahead

Through the years, much progress has been made in finding ways to decrease the amount of garbage that is generated. Major companies are committed to reducing the content and weight of packaging in order to cut the volume of waste, and many have made significant progress in this area. Individuals and businesses are putting the concept of reuse into practice so items that are still usable do not end up in landfills. Recycling continues to grow in popularity, but is often viewed by environmental groups as a last resort, with eliminating waste up front seen as the best solution. Technology is also playing an important role by making it possible to convert landfill waste into fuel and electricity. With these solutions, and others that will undoubtedly be conceived in the future, the world's garbage problems may someday be much less of a challenge than they are today.

How Can Garbage Be Reduced in the Future?

66 This is not an incineration process that creates greenhouse gases, hazardous ash, and other air pollutants. The intense heat of the plasma gasification process actually rearranges the molecular structure of the waste, transforming organic (carbon-based) materials into an ultra-clean, synthetic gas (syngas) rich in carbon and hydrogen. 99

—Jeffrey E. Surma, "Finding a Sustainable Future at the Dump," *Boston Globe*, January 12, 2009. www.boston.com.

Surma is president and CEO of InEnTec, an Oregon-based firm specializing in the conversion of waste into clean, renewable products.

66 Incinerators with names like 'gasification,' 'pyrolysis,' 'plasma arc,' and 'waste-to-energy' all emit dioxins and other harmful pollutants, despite industry claims that they are 'green' technologies. 99

—Global Alliance for Incinerator Alternatives, "Incinerators in Disguise," February 5, 2008. www.no-burn.org.

The Global Alliance for Incinerator Alternatives is a worldwide alliance of groups and individuals who are dedicated to a toxic-free world without incineration.

Bracketed quotes indicate conflicting positions.

* Editor's Note: While the definition of a primary source can be narrowly or broadly defined, for the purposes of Compact Research, a primary source consists of: 1) results of original research presented by an organization or researcher; 2) eyewitness accounts of events, personal experience, or work experience; 3) first-person editorials offering pundits' opinions; 4) government officials presenting political plans and/or policies; 5) representatives of organizations presenting testimony or policy.

Primary Source Quotes

❝Zero Waste maximizes recycling, minimizes waste, reduces consumption, and ensures that products are made to be reused, repaired, or recycled back into nature or the marketplace.❞

—Nicky Scott, *Reduce, Reuse, Recycle.* White River Junction, VT: Chelsea Green, 2007.

Scott is an author from the United Kingdom who writes about recycling and composting issues.

❝Despite the efforts of the zero-waste movement, which would eliminate landfills completely, landfills will still be needed for many years.❞

—John G. Carlton, "The Future of Landfill Planning: Reduce Waste," CDM, 2010. www.cdm.com.

Carlton is an environmental engineer from Massachusetts.

❝At first glance Zero Waste seems like an abstract, maybe even unattainable notion. But it is now being embraced, practiced, and accomplished in many corners of the world.❞

—Robin De Lill Stroman, "Is New York Ready for Zero Waste?" *Finger Lake Sierran,* Winter 2008. http://newyork.sierraclub.org.

Stroman is zero-waste committee chair of the Sierra Club's Finger Lakes Group in New York State.

66 Putting our bottles and paper in a blue bin just won't cut it. That doesn't mean we shouldn't do it, but let's get over all the hoopla about it. Yes, recycle. Of course, recycle. But don't believe for a second that recycling, alone, is enough to turn things around. 99

—Annie Leonard, "MoJo Forum: Is Recycling a Waste?" *Mother Jones*, April 20, 2009. http://motherjones.com.

Leonard is an environmental researcher and campaigner and the author and host of *The Story of Stuff,* an animated online exposé of the hidden costs of consumption.

66 If we continue on the same wasting path with rising per capita waste generation rates and stagnating recycling and composting rates, by the year 2030 Americans could generate 301 million tons per year of municipal solid waste, up from 251 million tons in 2006. 99

— Brenda Platt, David Ciplet, Kate M. Bailey, and Eric Lombardi, *Stop Trashing the Climate,* June 2008. www.stoptrashingtheclimate.com.

Platt is with the Institute for Local Self-Reliance, Ciplet is with the Global Anti-Incinerator Alliance, and Bailey and Lombardi are with Eco-Cycle.

66 The ultimate goal is to create products that can provide increased benefits to our society and our economy—on energy that is renewable, made of materials that are benign, and based on renewable and reusable feedstocks. 99

—Paul T. Anastas, "Hearing on E-Waste R&D Act," testimony before the U.S. House of Representatives Committee on Science and Technology, February 9, 2009. http://democrats.science.house.gov.

Anastas is with the Center for Green Chemistry and Green Engineering at Yale University.

How Can Garbage Be Reduced in the Future?

- The Aluminum Association states that the recycling rate for used aluminum beverage containers in the United States is **54 percent today**, and the goal for 2015 is **75 percent**.

- The British government has set goals for its recycling and composting rates of **45 percent** by 2015 and **50 percent** by 2020.

- According to calculations by the United Nations, by converting the world's landfill waste to biofuel, global carbon emissions would be reduced by an average of **58 percent** for every unit of energy produced.

- According to environmental engineer John G. Carlton, waste-to-energy technologies are capable of shrinking landfill waste to only **10 percent** of the initial volume.

- By 2020 the European Union will require member nations to reduce the amount of trash sent to landfills to **35 percent** of what it was in 1995.

- Walmart's goal is to accomplish **zero waste** by the year 2025 by reducing, recycling, or reusing all packaging that comes into its 4,100 American stores.

- In 2009 the H.J. Heinz Company announced its goal of cutting solid waste, energy use, greenhouse gas emissions, and water consumption by **20 percent** by the year 2015.

- By the year 2020, **Interface**, the largest carpet manufacturer in the world, has a goal of eliminating all forms of waste in every area of its business, including toxic substances from production, vehicles, and facilities.

- Boulder County, Colorado, plans to reduce its waste by **85 percent** by 2017, and in the following years its goal is to achieve **zero waste**.

Fewer Active Landfills

The number of landfills in the United States has declined dramatically over the years, either because they were full or failed to meet regulatory requirements. But since modern landfills are bigger than those of the past, the EPA states that overall capacity has remained relatively constant. Still, even though some states have plenty of capacity left, others have none, and must transport their garbage to other states. This graph shows the decline in U.S. landfills between 1988 and 2007.

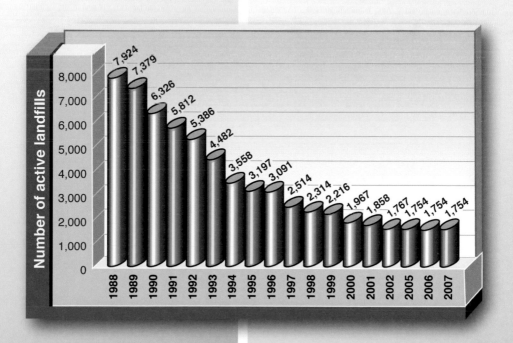

Source: Environmental Protection Agency, *Municipal Solid Waste Generation, Recycling, and Disposal in the United States: Facts and Figures for 2007*, November 2008. www.epa.gov.

Vaporizing Garbage

Many waste management experts tout the value of plasma gasification as a solution for garbage reduction, as well as a way for the world to wean itself from fossil fuels. The process involves heating landfill waste (or other carbon-containing materials) to temperatures that are nearly as hot as the sun's surface. This process breaks down the molecular structure of the waste and converts it into synthetic gas known as syngas. The gas can then be used to generate electrical power, as well as to make liquid fuels or other sustainable sources of energy. This illustration shows how the plasma gasification process works.

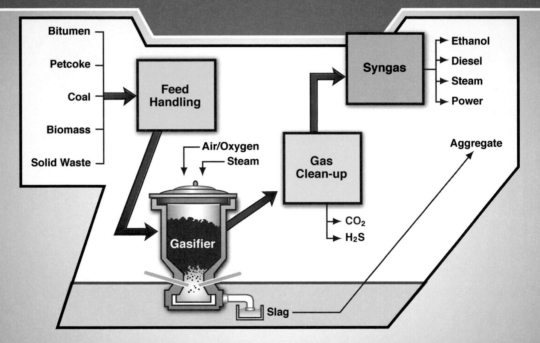

*Note: Waste and other materials that can be converted into electricity or fuels are known as feedstocks.

Source: Westinghouse Plasma Corporation, "What Is Plasma Gasification?" 2010. www.westinghouse-plasma.com.

- A recycling initiative by America's largest plastic bag makers calls for the use of **40 percent** recycled content in the bags by 2015, which will be the equivalent of using **36 billion** recycled plastic bags to make new bags.

- The European Union requires that all its member nations reduce trash thrown into landfills by **50 percent** by 2015, and those who do not comply risk being assessed millions of dollars in fines.

- A report published in May 2009 by Pike Research showed that the worldwide electronic waste crisis will continue to worsen until 2015, and then global volume will begin to decline due to the implementation of key **e-waste initiatives**.

Key People and Advocacy Groups

Aluminum Association: An organization that represents producers of aluminum and fabricated products, aluminum recyclers, and industry suppliers.

Container Recycling Institute: An organization that studies and promotes policies and programs that increase recovery and recycling of beverage containers to minimize their impact on the environment.

Earth911: An environmental services company that addresses waste and recycling solutions for businesses and consumers.

Environment Technology Council: An organization that advocates strong environmental standards to ensure the proper management of hazardous waste and to achieve a balance between the environment and the economy.

Global Alliance for Incinerator Alternatives: A worldwide alliance of groups and individuals dedicated to a toxic-free world without incineration.

International Solid Waste Association: An international nonprofit organization that works to promote and develop sustainable waste management practices worldwide.

NPTA Alliance: The trade association for the paper, packaging, and supplies distribution industry.

National Recycling Coalition: An organization that advocates sound management practices for raw materials in an effort to eliminate waste and promote sustainable economies.

National Solid Wastes Management Association: A trade association representing North American companies that provide waste collection, recycling, and disposal services.

Sierra Club: A grassroots environmental organization that works to protect communities, wild places, and the planet itself.

Society of the Plastics Industry: The trade association representing the plastics manufacturing industry.

Solid Waste Association of North America: An organization that seeks to advance environmentally and economically sound management of municipal solid waste in North America.

U.S. Environmental Protection Agency: An agency of the federal government that is dedicated to protecting human health and the environment

Chronology

1890
The British Paper Company is established specifically to make paper and board from recycled materials.

1834
A law enacted in Charleston, West Virginia, protects vultures from hunters because the birds help eat the city's garbage.

1904
America's first two major aluminum recycling plants open in Cleveland and Chicago.

1933
Communities on the New Jersey shoreline obtain a court order that forces New York City to stop dumping garbage in the Atlantic Ocean.

1878
The mayor of Memphis, Tennessee, organizes garbage collection at homes and businesses using small, mule-drawn wooden carts.

1850   1875   1900   1925   1950

1864
Health officials in Memphis, Tennessee, speculate that there may be a connection between the spread of yellow fever and garbage being dumped throughout the city. To mitigate this threat, city officials instruct residents to dump their garbage at specific locations on the edge of town.

1898
The first recycling facility in the United States opens in New York City and recovers up to 37 percent of the waste from more than 116,000 residents.

1959
The American Society of Civil Engineers publishes a standard guide to sanitary landfills, which suggests that garbage be compacted and covered with soil each day to guard against foul odor and infestation by rodents.

1934
The U.S. Supreme Court bans the common practice of dumping municipal waste into the ocean, but its ruling does not apply to commercial or industrial waste.

1918
Cities throughout the United States begin switching from horse-drawn to motorized refuse collection equipment.

1970
The Clean Air Act becomes law and leads to the closure of many waste incinerators for their ineffectiveness at controlling air pollution. The U.S. Environmental Protection Agency is created the same year.

2002
New York City's Fresh Kills landfill is filled to capacity and is closed. The parks and recreation department announces a plan to convert the site into one of the country's largest city parks.

1973
The first U.S. curbside recycling program is implemented in Berkeley, California.

1979
The U.S. Environmental Protection Agency issues landfill criteria that prohibit open dumping.

1990
A total of 140 recycling laws are in place in 38 U.S. states and the District of Columbia.

2010
A team of scientists discovers an enormous garbage patch in the Atlantic Ocean.

1970   1980   1990   2000   2010

1987
An Islip, Long Island, garbage barge known as *Mobro 4000* hauls the same load of trash up and down the Atlantic coast. After the garbage is rejected by six states and three countries, it is eventually incinerated in Brooklyn, New York, and the ash is disposed of in a landfill.

2007
San Francisco becomes the first city in the United States to outlaw the distribution of plastic bags by grocery stores.

1971
Oregon becomes the first state to introduce a "bottle bill," which requires a refundable deposit of 5 cents on beer and soda bottles as an incentive to promote recycling.

2009
The Aluminum Association, Can Manufacturers Institute, and Institute of Scrap Recycling Industries officially announce that the recycling rate for aluminum cans exceeded 54 percent in 2008, the highest of all beverage containers.

Related Organizations

Clean Air Council

135 S. Nineteenth St., Suite 300
Philadelphia, PA 19103
phone: (215) 567-4004
fax: (215) 567-5791
Web site: www.cleanair.org

The Clean Air Council is an environmental organization that is dedicated to everyone's right to breathe clean air. Its Web site has a section devoted to waste reduction and recycling that offers waste facts and figures, statistics, information about electronic waste, and links to other environmental organizations.

Container Recycling Institute

89 E. Lake Shore Trail
Glastonbury, CT 06033
phone: (202) 263-0999
e-mail: info@container-recycling.org • Web site: www.container-re cycling.org

The Container Recycling Institute studies and promotes policies and programs that increase recovery and recycling of beverage containers to minimize their impact on the environment. Its Web site features facts and statistics about recycling aluminum, plastic, and glass; current issues; a newsletter and other online publications; and a "Just for Kids" section.

Earth911

1375 N. Scottsdale Rd., Suite 360
Scottsdale, AZ 85257
phone: (480) 889-2650
Web site: http://earth911.com

Earth911 is an environmental services company that addresses waste and recycling solutions for businesses and consumers. Its Web site features news articles, a "Recycling 101" section with an extensive array of recycling-related publications, a weekly newsletter, and a "News and Lifestyle" section with articles about current issues.

Environmental Technology Council (ETC)

734 Fifteenth St. NW, Suite 720
Washington, DC 20005-1013
phone: (202) 783-0870
fax: (202) 737-2038
e-mail: comments@etc.org • Web site: www.etc.org

The ETC advocates strong environmental standards to ensure the proper management of hazardous waste and to achieve a balance between the environment and the economy. The Web site's "Hazardous Waste Resource Center" link offers a "What Is Hazardous Waste" section, technology and environment issues, treatment methods, chemicals of concern, and information about environmental legislation.

Global Alliance for Incinerator Alternatives (GAIA)

1958 University Ave.
Berkeley, CA 94704
phone: (510) 883-9490
fax: (510) 883-9493
e-mail: info@no-burn.org
Web site: www.no-burn.org

The GAIA is a worldwide alliance of groups and individuals who are dedicated to a toxic-free world without incineration. Its Web site features information on campaigns to promote recycling and raise awareness of other environmental causes, an extensive section devoted to current issues, a "Solutions" section, and a number of fact sheets, news articles, and other publications.

International Solid Waste Association (ISWA)

Auerspergstrasse 15, Top 41
1080 Vienna
Austria
phone: +(431) 253 6001
e-mail: iswa@iswa.org • Web site: www.iswa.org
The ISWA is an international nonprofit organization that works to promote and develop sustainable waste management practices worldwide.

Its Web site features numerous publications about waste and recycling, position papers, technical policy papers, and abstracts of waste management and research articles.

Keep America Beautiful

1010 Washington Blvd.
Stamford, CT 06901
phone: (203) 659-3000
fax: (203) 659-3001
e-mail: info@kab.org • Web site: www.kab.org

The mission of Keep America Beautiful is to engage individuals to take greater responsibility for improving their community environments. Its Web site offers a section devoted to waste reduction and recycling. It publishes a quarterly newsletter called *Bin Buzz* and a fact sheet that shows cleanup and recycling results.

National Recycling Coalition

805 Fifteenth St. NW, Suite 425
Washington, DC 20005
phone: (202) 789-1430
fax: (202) 789-1431
e-mail: info@nrc-recycle.org • Web site: www.nrc-recycle.org

The National Recycling Coalition advocates sound management practices for raw materials in an effort to eliminate waste and promote sustainable economies. Its Web site offers archived news releases, news articles, and a section devoted to recycling.

National Solid Wastes Management Association (NSWMA)

4301 Connecticut Ave. NW, Suite 300
Washington, DC 20008
phone: (202) 244-4700; toll free: (800) 424-2869
fax: (202) 966-4824
Web site: www.environmentalistseveryday.org

The NSWMA is a trade association representing North American companies that provide waste collection, recycling, and disposal services. Its Web site offers information on the history of solid waste management, current research and statistics, a news article archive, and a "Profiles in Garbage" section with fact sheets about items that are part of the waste stream.

The Nature Conservancy

Worldwide Office
4245 N. Fairfax Dr., Suite 100
Arlington, VA 22203-1606
phone: (703) 841-5300
Web site: www.nature.org

The Nature Conservancy is a conservation organization that works worldwide to protect the environment on behalf of people and nature. Its Web site offers news releases, inspirational stories, information about current initiatives, a search engine that produces articles on garbage and recycling, and a link to the Cool Green Science blog.

Sierra Club

85 Second St., 2nd Floor
San Francisco, CA 94105
phone: (415) 977-5500
fax: (415) 977-5799
e-mail: info@sierraclub.org • Web site: www.sierraclub.org

The Sierra Club is a grassroots environmental organization that works to protect communities, wild places, and the planet itself. Its Web site features news articles, links to several different blogs, and a search engine that produces numerous publications about garbage and recycling.

Solid Waste Association of North America (SWANA)

1100 Wayne Ave., Suite 700
Silver Spring, MD 20910
phone: (800) 467-9262
fax: (301) 589-7068
Web site: www.swana.org

SWANA seeks to advance environmentally and economically sound management of municipal solid waste in North America. Its Web site's search engine produces a number of articles related to garbage and recycling.

U.S. Environmental Protection Agency (EPA)

Ariel Rios Building
1200 Pennsylvania Ave. NW
Washington, DC 20460
phone: (202) 272-0167
Web site: www.epa.gov

The EPA's mission is to protect human health and the environment. Its Web site features news releases, research topics, a "Science and Technology" section, and a search engine that brings up a wide variety of articles related to garbage and recycling.

For Further Research

Books

Lori Baird, *Don't Throw It Out: Recycle, Renew, and Reuse to Make Things Last*. New York: Rodale, 2007.

Lauri S. Friedman, ed., *Garbage and Recycling*. Farmington Hills, MI: Greenhaven, 2009.

Anne Maczulak, *Waste Treatment: Reducing Global Waste*. New York: Facts On File, 2009.

Nicky Scott, *Reduce, Reuse, Recycle. An Easy Household Guide*. White River Junction, VT: Chelsea Green, 2007.

Tristram Stuart, *Waste: Uncovering the Global Food Scandal*. New York: Norton, 2009.

Robert and Susanne E. Vandenbosch, *Nuclear Waste Stalemate: Political and Scientific Controversies*. Salt Lake City: University of Utah Press, 2007.

Sim Van der Ryn, *The Toilet Papers: Recycling Waste and Conserving Water*. White River Junction, VT: Chelsea Green, 2008.

Kate Walker, *Food and Garden Waste*. New York: Marshall Cavendish Benchmark, 2010.

Periodicals

John Coté, "S.F. OKs Toughest Recycling Law in U.S.," *San Francisco Chronicle*, June 10, 2009.

Monica Eng, "Chicago Schools Pile Up Lunch Waste," *Chicago Tribune*, February 7, 2010.

Chrissy Kadleck, "Family Recycling Biz Turns Garbage to Gold," *Waste & Recycling News*, September 28, 2009.

Leslie Kaufman, "Nudging Recycling from Less Waste to None," *New York Times*, October 29, 2009.

Bill McKibben, "Waste Not, Want Not," *Mother Jones*, May/June 2009.

Jesse McKinley, "In a California Town, Birth Defects, Deaths and Questions," *New York Times*, February 7, 2010.

Chaz Miller, "The Garbage Barge," *Waste Age*, February 1, 2007.

Jane Anne Morris, "Is Recycling the New Garbage?" *Synthesis/Regeneration*, Spring 2008.

Keith Naughton and Daniel McGinn, "Saving the World for a Latte," *Newsweek*, October 6, 2008.

Christine Negroni, "Leaving the Trash Behind," *New York Times*, February 22, 2010.

Elisabeth Rosenthal, "Smuggling Europe's Waste to Poorer Countries," *New York Times*, September 26, 2009.

William Sherman, "Confusion, Lack of Space Discourage New Yorkers from Recycling More," *New York Daily News*, October 4, 2009.

Daniel Stone, "Can the Pacific Garbage Patch Be Cleaned Up?" *Newsweek*, January 19, 2010.

Bryan Walsh, "Making Recycling Really Pay," *Time*, April 11, 2008.

———, "Meet Dave, the Man Who Never Takes Out the Trash," *Time*, September 22, 2008.

Internet Sources

BioCycle, "The State of Garbage in America," December 2008. www.jgpress.com/archives/_free/001782.html.

Anthony Bradley, "Recycling Is for the Gullible," Acton Institute, August 20, 2008. http://bradley.chattablogs.com/archives/2008/08/recycling-myth.html.

Ed Grabianowski, "How Recycling Works," *HowStuffWorks*, 2007. http://science.howstuffworks.com/recycling2.htm.

Brenda Platt, David Ciplet, Kate M. Bailey, and Eric Lombardi, *Stop Trashing the Climate*, June 2008. www.stoptrashingtheclimate.com/fullreport_stoptrashingtheclimate.pdf.

Sylvia Poggioli, "Naples, Italy, Trashed by Garbage Crisis," NPR, January 11, 2008. www.npr.org/templates/story/story.php?storyId=18017044.

U.S. Environmental Protection Agency, *Municipal Solid Waste Generation, Recycling, and Disposal in the United States: Facts and Figures for 2008*, November 2009. www.epa.gov/osw/nonhaz/municipal/pubs/msw2008rpt.pdf.

Source Notes

Overview

1. Steve Cohen, "Wasted: New York City's Giant Garbage Problem," *New York Observer*, April 3, 2008. www.observer.com.
2. Cohen, "Wasted."
3. Beyond Pest Control, "New York City's Rat Complaints Are Up Despite Concentrated Efforts from the City," 2009. www.nypestpro.com.
4. Keith Bradsher, "China's Incinerators Loom as a Global Hazard," *New York Times*, August 12, 2009. www.nytimes.com.
5. Elisabeth Rosenthal, "The Incinerator as Eye Candy," *New York Times*, April 13, 2010. http://green.blogs.nytimes.com.
6. Russell McLendon, "What Is the Great Pacific Ocean Garbage Patch?" *Mother Nature Network*, September 8, 2009. www.mnn.com.
7. U.S. Environmental Protection Agency, *Municipal Solid Waste Generation, Recycling, and Disposal in the United States: Facts and Figures for 2008*, November 2009. www.epa.gov.
8. Jane Kay, "S.F.'s Scraps Bring Joy to Area Farmers," *San Francisco Chronicle*, April 1, 2009. http://articles.sfgate.com.
9. Quoted in Andi McDaniel, "Can We Create a World Without Waste?" AlterNet, January 9, 2007. www.alternet.org.
10. Westinghouse Plasma Corporation, "Environmental Benefits," 2007. www.westinghouse-plasma.com.

How Serious a Problem Is Garbage?

11. Alexander Smoltczyk, Andreas Ulrich, and Andreas Wassermann, "The Garbage of Naples: How the Mafia Helped Send Italy's Trash to Germany," *Spiegel International*, March 24, 2010. www.spiegel.de.
12. Quoted in Elisabeth Rosenthal, "All of Europe Getting a Whiff of Naples Garbage Problem," *New York Times*, June 8, 2008. www.nytimes.com.
13. U.S. Environmental Protection Agency, "10 Fast Facts on Recycling," February 25, 2010. www.epa.gov.
14. *Environment News Service*, "Landfill Methane Awards: From Greenhouse Gas to Energy Source," January 13, 2010. www.ens-newswire.com.
15. Elisabeth Rosenthal, "Europe Finds Clean Energy in Trash, But U.S. Lags," *New York Times*, April 12, 2010. www.nytimes.com.
16. Rosenthal, "Europe Finds Clean Energy in Trash, But U.S. Lags."
17. Leo Hickman, "Do We Really Need to Ban Plastic Bags?" *Guardian*, August 11, 2009. www.guardian.co.uk.

Is Toxic Garbage a Serious Problem?

18. Yamaha Gong, "Family Thrives Yet Doubts in Pollution Town," MyShantou, April 2, 2008. http://news.myshantou.net.
19. Quoted in Bryan Walsh, "E-Waste Not," *Time*, January 8, 2009. www.time.com.
20. Quoted in *60 Minutes*, "Following the Trail of Toxic E-Waste," CBS News, November 9, 2008. www.cbsnews.com.
21. Sierra Club Zero Waste Committee, "Zero Waste Cradle-to-Cradle Principles for the 21st Century: Municipal Solid Waste Landfills," September 2009. www.sierraclubmass.org.

22. Quoted in Elizabeth Shogren, "CFL Bulbs Have One Hitch: Toxic Mercury," NPR, February 15, 2007. www.npr.org.

23. Quoted in *Environment News Service*, "Enviros in Court to Defend EPA Medical Waste Incinerator Rule," January 7, 2010. www.ens-newswire.com.

24. Quoted in *Environment News Service*, "Enviros in Court to Defend EPA Medical Waste Incinerator Rule."

25. Charles Moore, "Across the Pacific Ocean, Plastics, Plastics, Everywhere," Mindfully, November 2003. www.mindfully.org.

26. Quoted in Mike Melia, "Atlantic Garbage Patch: Pacific Gyre Is Not Alone," *Huffington Post*, April 15, 2010. www.huffingtonpost.com.

27. Quoted in Kathy Marks, "The World's Rubbish Dump: A Tip That Stretches from Hawaii to Japan," *Independent*, February 5, 2008. www.independent.co.uk.

How Effective Is Recycling?

28. Quoted in Laura Casey, "Teardown House Becomes Recycling Success Story," *Seattle Times*, June 7, 2009. http://seattletimes.nwsource.com.

29. Natural Resources Defense Council, "The Past, Present and Future of Recycling," March 28, 2008. www.nrdc.org.

30. Chaz Miller, "Myth Bluster," *Waste Age*, February 1, 2008. http://wasteage.com.

31. Miller, "Myth Bluster."

32. Alcoa Recycling, "U.S. Aluminum Can Recycling Reached 54.2 Percent in 2008," August 13, 2009. http://alcoa.typepad.com.

33. Quoted in Emilie Rusch, "Recycling 'Makes Economic Sense,'" *Rapid City Journal*, January 17, 2010. www.rapidcityjournal.com.

34. Amanda Ruggeri, "Could the Recession Kill the Recycling Industry?" *U.S. News & World Report*, January 14, 2010. www.usnews.com.

How Can Garbage Be Reduced in the Future?

35. Joseph Brinker, "Out of the Garbage-Pail into the Fire," *Popular Science Monthly*, February 1919. http://books.google.com.

36. CalRecycle, "Waste Reduction," November 23, 2009. www.calrecycle.ca.gov.

37. Frito-Lay, "Reduce, Reuse, Recycle," 2010. www.fritolay.com.

38. *Waco Tribune*, "Hey Waco: Let's Freecycle," editorial, January 11, 2010. www.wacotrib.com.

39. Rethink Initiative, "EBay and Fellow Members of the Rethink Initiative Are Applying Some Fresh Thinking to the Problem of E-Waste." http://pages.ebay.com.

40. Quoted in Eartheasy, "EBay Launches PC Reuse and Recycling Initiative." www.eartheasy.com.

41. Quoted in Jason Dearen, "Trash to Gas: Landfill Energy Projects Increasing," *Seattle Times*, January 5, 2010. http://seattletimes.nwsource.com.

List of Illustrations

Index

Note: Boldface page numbers refer to illustrations.